1000 things you should know about

plants

John Farndon

Miles Kelly

PUBLISHING

This material was first published as hardback in 2000

This edition published in 2007 by Miles Kelly Publishing Ltd
Bardfield Centre, Great Bardfield, Essex, CM7 4SL

2 4 6 8 10 9 7 5 3 1

Editorial Director: Belinda Gallagher
Art Director: Jo Brewer
Volume Designer: Ian Paulyn
Picture Researchers: Jennifer Hunt, Liberty Newton
Reprographics: Anthony Cambray, Stephan Davis,
Liberty Newton, Ian Paulyn

British Library Cataloguing-in-Publication Data
A catalogue record for this book is available from the British Library

ISBN 978- 1-84236-819-0

Printed in China

info@mileskelly.net
www.mileskelly.net

All artworks from the MKP Archives

The publishers would like to thank the following sources
for the use of their photographs:
Page 10 (T/L) Jo Brewer; Page 14 (T/R) Gunter Marx/CORBIS;
Page 19 (T/R) Bob Gibbons/Holt Studios; Page 19 (B/L) Jo Brewer;
Page 24 (T/R) Woflgang Kaehler/CORBIS; Page 25 (T/R) Jo Brewer;
Page 28 (B/C) John Holmes, Frank Lane Picture Agency/CORBIS;
Page 29 (B/L) Jo Brewer; Page 35 (T/L) Richard T. Nowitz/CORBIS;
Page 38 (T/R) Jo Brewer; Page 38 (B/L) Steve Austin, Papilio/CORBIS;
Page 46 (T/R) Wayne Lawler, Ecoscene/CORBIS; Page 48 (B/L)
Sally A. Morgan, Ecoscene/CORBIS; Page 51 (B/R) Douglas P. Wilson,
Frank Lane Picture Agency/CORBIS; Page 61 (T/R) Dennis McGuire

All other photographs from:
Castrol, CMCD, Corbis, Corel, digitalSTOCK, digitalvision,
Flat Earth, Hemera, ILN, John Foxx, PhotoAlto, PhotoDisc,
PhotoEssentials, PhotoPro, Stockbyte

1000 things you should know about

plants

CONTENTS

Perennial flowers

▲ *Chrysanthemums are among the most popular perennials.*

● **Garden perennials** are flowers that live for at least three years.

● **Perennials** may not bloom in the first year, but after that they bloom every year.

● **Since they bloom** for many years, perennials do not need to produce as many seeds to survive.

● **Some perennials** are herbaceous – that is, they have soft stems. The stems wither at the end of each summer and new stems grow next spring.

● **Woody perennials** have woody stems. Their stems don't wither, but most shed their leaves in autumn.

● **Perennials** from temperate (cool) regions, like asters, irises, lupins, wallflowers, peonies and primroses, need a cold winter to encourage new buds to grow in spring.

● **Tropical perennials** such as African violets, begonias and gloxinias cannot survive winters outdoors in temperate climates.

● **Most perennials** spread by sending out shoots from their roots which develop into new stems.

● **Some perennials** such as columbines and delphiniums last for only three or four years.

● **Gardeners** spread perennials by taking cuttings – that is, pieces cut from stems or roots.

Oak trees

● **Oaks** are a group of over 450 different trees. Most belong to a family with the Latin name *Quercus*.

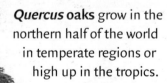

● ***Quercus* oaks** grow in the northern half of the world in temperate regions or high up in the tropics.

● **Southern oaks,** such as the Australian and Tasmanian oaks, don't belong to the *Quercus* family.

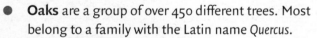

◀ *Oaks have leaves with four or five pairs of lobes. They grow fruits called acorns in a little cup.*

★ STAR FACT ★
The bark of cork oaks in Portugal and Spain is made into corks for bottles.

● **Most oaks** from warmer places, such as the holm oak, are evergreen.

● **When a nail** is driven into freshly cut oak, it creates a blue stain as tannin in the wood reacts with the iron.

● **Tannin from oak bark** has been used for curing leather since the days of ancient Greece.

● **Oak trees** can live a thousand years or more and grow up to 40 m. In Europe, oaks are the oldest of all trees.

● **Oak wood** is very strong and durable and so was the main building wood for centuries – used for timber frames in houses and for building ships.

● **Oak trees** are divided into white oaks like the English oak and red oaks like the North American pine oak according to the colour of their wood.

Spices

- **The Phoenicians** traded in spices 2500 years ago.

- **The great voyages** of exploration of the 1400s, like those of Columbus, were mainly to find ways to reach sources of spices in southeast Asia.

- **The Molucca Islands** in Indonesia were known as the Spice Islands because they were the main source of cloves, nutmeg and mace.

- **Sesame** was used by the ancient Chinese for ink and by the Romans as sandwich spread. Arabs thought it had magical powers. In *Ali Baba and the 40 Thieves*, Ali says, 'open sesame' to magically open a door.

- **Cinnamon** is the inner bark of a laurel tree native to Sri Lanka. It was once more valuable than gold.

▲ *Spices made from fragrant tropical plants have long been used to flavour food.*

- **Allspice** is the berries of a myrtle tree native to the West Indies. It gets its name because it tastes like a mixture of cloves, cinnamon and nutmeg.

- **In ancient Greece and Rome** people often paid their taxes in peppercorns.

- **Cloves are the dried buds** of a large evergreen tree that grows in the Moluccas.

- **From 200 BC** Chinese courtiers sucked cloves to make their breath smell sweet for the Emperor.

- **Saffron** is the yellow stigmas of the purple saffron crocus, used as a dye by Buddhist priests. It is the most costly of all spices. It takes 170,000 flowers to make just 1 kg.

Marine plants

- **Plants in the sea** can only live in the sunlit surface waters of the ocean, called the photic zone.

- **The photic zone** goes down about 100 m.

- **Phytoplankton** are minute, floating, plant-like organisms made from just a single cell.

- **Almost any marine plant** big enough to be seen with the naked eye is called seaweed.

- **Seaweeds** are anchored by 'holdfasts' that look like roots but are really suckers for holding on to rocks.

- **Seaweeds** are red, green or brown algae. Red algae are small and fern-like and grow 30–60 m down in tropical seas. Brown algae like giant kelp are big and grow down to about 20 m, mostly in cold water.

- **Some seaweeds** such as the bladderwrack have gas pockets to help their fronds (leaves) float.

- **The fastest growing** plant in the sea is the giant kelp, which can grow 1 m in a single day. Giant kelp can grow up to 60 m long.

- **The Sargasso Sea** is a vast area of sea covering 5.2 million sq km east of the West Indies. Gulfweed floats so densely here that it looks like green meadows.

- **The Sargasso Sea** was discovered by Christopher Columbus in 1492.

◄ *Seaweeds don't have roots, stems, leaves or flowers, but they are plants and make their food from sunlight (see photosynthesis).*

Gardens

- **The ancient Chinese and Greeks** grew fruit trees, vegetables and herbs in gardens for food and for medicines.
- **In the 1500s** there were five famous botanical gardens in Europe designed to study and grow herbs for medicine.
- **The first botanical gardens** were at Pisa (1543) and Padua (1545) in Italy.
- **Carolus Clusius** set up a famous flower garden in Leiden in Holland in the late 1500s. Here the first tulips from China were grown and the Dutch bulb industry began.
- **The most famous gardener** of the 17th century was John Evelyn who set up a beautiful garden at Sayes Court in Deptford near London.
- **The Royal Botanic Gardens** at Kew near London were made famous by Sir Joseph Banks in the late 1700s for their collections of plants from around the world.

◄ *Gardening has become one of the most popular of all pastimes.*

- **Today Kew Gardens** has 33,400 classes of living plants and a herbarium of dried plants with 7 million species – that's 98 percent of the world's plants.
- **Plants** such as rubber plants, pineapples, bananas, tea and coffee were spread around the world from Kew.
- **Lancelot 'Capability' Brown** (1716–83) was a famous English landscape gardener. He got his nickname by telling clients their gardens had excellent 'capabilities'.
- **Ornamental gardens** are ordinary flower gardens.

Cones

- **Cones** are the tough little clusters of scales that coniferous trees carry their seeds in.
- **The scales** on a cone are called bracts. The seeds are held between the bracts. Bracts are thin and papery in spruces and thick and woody in silver firs.
- **Pine cone bracts** have a lump called an umbo.
- **All cones** are green and quite soft when they first form, then turn brown and hard as they ripen.
- **Cones stand upright** on the branch until they are ripe and ready to shed their seeds.
- **Most cones** turn over when ripe to hang downwards so that the seeds fall out.
- **The cones of cedars** and silver firs stay upright and the bracts drop away to release the seeds.

- **Long, hanging cones** like those of the pine and spruce hang throughout winter then release seeds in spring.
- **The monkey puzzle** tree has a unique, pineapple-shaped cone with golden spines and edible seeds.

▼ *These Scots pine cones are brown and were fertilized about three years ago. Younger cones further out on branches would have been fertilized last spring and would still be green.*

Lichen

- **Lichens** are a remarkable partnership between algae and fungi.
- **The algae** in lichen are tiny green balls that make the food from sunlight to feed the fungi.
- **The fungi make a protective** layer around the algae and hold water.
- **There are 20,000** species of lichen. Some grow on soil, but most grow on rocks or tree bark.
- **Fruticose lichens** are shrub-like, foliose lichens look like leaves, and crustose lichens look like crusts.
- **Lichens only grow** when moistened by rain.
- **Lichens can survive** in many places where other plants would die, such as the Arctic, in deserts and on mountain tops.
- **Some Arctic lichens** are over 4000 years old.
- **Lichens are very sensitive** to air pollution, especially sulphur dioxide, and are used by scientists to indicate air pollution.

▲ *Lichens are tiny and slow-growing – some growing only a fraction of a millimetre a year. But they are usually long-lived.*

- **The oakmoss lichen** from Europe and North Africa is added to most perfumes and after-shaves to stop flower scents fading. Scandinavian reindeer moss is a lichen eaten by reindeer. It is exported to Germany for decorations.

Spores and seeds

▶ *New sycamore trees grow from their tiny winged seeds (top). Mushrooms (below right) grow from spores.*

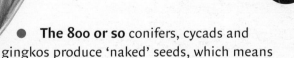

- **Seed plants** are plants that grow from seeds that are kept in the part of the plant called a fruit.
- **Seeds** have a tiny baby plant inside called an embryo from which the plant grows plus a supply of stored food and a protective coating.
- **Spores contain** special cells which grow into new organisms. Green plants, such as ferns and mosses, and fungi, such as mushrooms, produce spores.
- **All 250,000 flowering plants** produce 'enclosed' seeds. These are seeds that grow inside sacs called ovaries which turn into a fruit around the seed.

- **The 800 or so** conifers, cycads and gingkos produce 'naked' seeds, which means there is no fruit around them.
- **Seeds** only develop when a plant is fertilized by pollen.
- **The largest seeds** are those of the double coconut or coco-de-mer of the Seychelles which can sometimes weigh up to 20 kg.
- **Thirty thousand orchid seeds** weigh barely 1 gm.
- **The world's biggest tree**, the giant redwood, grows from tiny seeds that are less than 2 mm long.
- **Coconut trees** produce only a few big seeds; orchids produce millions, but only a few grow into plants.

Parts of a tree

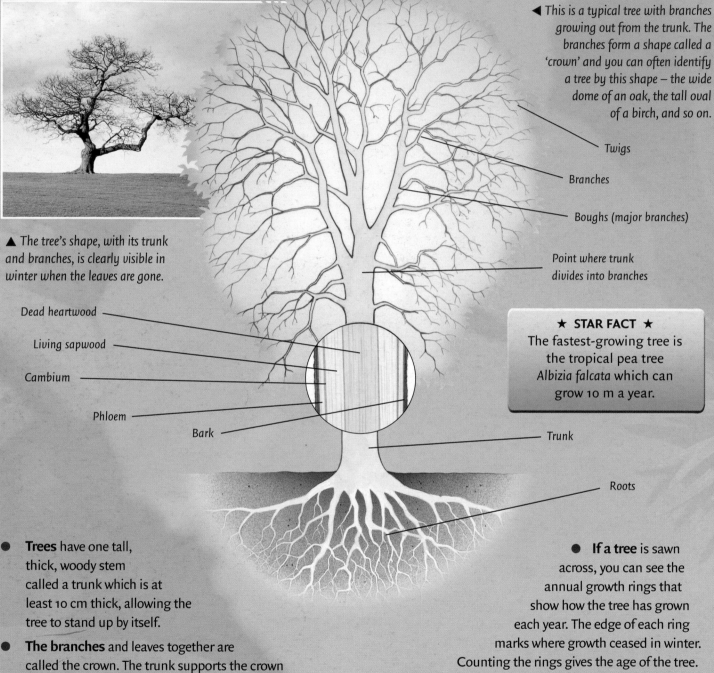

◀ This is a typical tree with branches growing out from the trunk. The branches form a shape called a 'crown' and you can often identify a tree by this shape – the wide dome of an oak, the tall oval of a birch, and so on.

Twigs

Branches

Boughs (major branches)

Point where trunk divides into branches

▲ The tree's shape, with its trunk and branches, is clearly visible in winter when the leaves are gone.

Dead heartwood

Living sapwood

Cambium

Phloem

Bark

★ STAR FACT ★
The fastest-growing tree is the tropical pea tree *Albizia falcata* which can grow 10 m a year.

Trunk

Roots

- **Trees** have one tall, thick, woody stem called a trunk which is at least 10 cm thick, allowing the tree to stand up by itself.

- **The branches** and leaves together are called the crown. The trunk supports the crown and holds it up to the sun.

- **The trunks of conifers** typically grow right to the top of the tree. The lower branches are longer because they have been growing longest. The upper branches are short because they are new. So the tree has a conical shape.

- **Trees with wide flat leaves** are called broad-leaved trees. They usually have crowns with a rounded shape.

- **The trunk and branches** have five layers from the centre out: heartwood, sapwood, cambium, phloem and bark.

- **If a tree** is sawn across, you can see the annual growth rings that show how the tree has grown each year. The edge of each ring marks where growth ceased in winter. Counting the rings gives the age of the tree.

- **Heartwood** is the dark, dead wood in the centre of the trunk. Sapwood is pale living wood, where tiny pipes called xylem carry sap from the roots to the leaves.

- **The cambium** is the thin layer where the sapwood is actually growing; the phloem is the thin food-conducting layer.

- **The bark** is the tree's protective skin of hard dead tissue. Bark takes many different forms and often cracks as the tree grows, but it is always made from cork.

Roses

- **The rose** is one of the most popular of all garden flowers because of its lovely perfume and beautiful blooms.

- **Wild roses** usually have small flowers and have a single layer of five petals. Garden roses usually have big flowers with multiple sets of five petals in two or more layers.

- **There are 100 species** of wild rose, but all today's garden roses were created by crossing 10 Asian species.

- **There are now over 13,000** official varieties of garden rose altogether.

- **Some experts divide garden roses** into groups by when they bloom: old roses bloom once a year in early summer; perpetual roses bloom in early summer, then again in autumn; and everblooming hybrids bloom all summer.

- **Old roses** include yellow briers, damask roses and many climbing roses.

- **Perpetuals** include what are called hybrid perpetuals.

- **Everblooming hybrids** include floribundas, hybrid teas, gloribundas and polyanthas.

▶ Roses often look their best just after they begin to open, when the petals are still in a tight, velvety cluster.

- **Hybrid teas** such as the Peace are the most popular of all roses. They were created by crossing everblooming but fragile tea roses with vigorous hybrid perpetuals.

- **Attar of roses** is a perfume made from roses, especially damask roses.

Rice

- **Rice** is a cereal grain that is the basic food of half the world's population. It is especially important in SE Asia.

- **The wild rice** or Indian rice collected by North American Indians for thousands of years is not related to rice.

- **Like other cereals**, rice is a grass, but it grows best in shallow water in tropical areas.

- **Rice growers** usually flood their fields to keep them wet. The flooded fields are called paddies.

★ STAR FACT ★
A lot of wheat is fed to livestock, but 95 percent of all rice is eaten by people.

- **The rice seeds** are sown in soil, then when the seedlings are 25–50 days old they are transplanted to the paddy field under 5–10 cm of water.

- **Brown rice** is rice grain with the husk ground away. White rice is rice grain with the inner bran layer ground away as well, and is far less nutritious.

- **Rice-growing** probably began in India about 3000BC.

- **In 1962** researchers in the Philippines experimented with hybrids of 10,000 strains of rice. They made a rice called 'IR-8' by crossing a tall, vigorous rice from Indonesia and a dwarf rice from Taiwan.

- **IR-8** sometimes gave double yields, and was called 'miracle rice', but it did not grow well in poor soils.

◀ To keep paddies flooded, fields on hillsides are banked in terraces.

Mushrooms

▲ Like other fungi, mushrooms cannot make their own food and feed off hosts such as trees.

- **Mushrooms** are umbrella-shaped fungi, many of which are edible.

- **Mushrooms** feed off either living or decaying plants.

- **Poisonous mushrooms** are called toadstools.

- **The umbrella-shaped** part of the mushroom is called the fruiting body. Under the surface is a mass of fine stalk threads called the mycelium.

- **The threads** making up the mycelium are called hyphae (said hi-fi). These absorb food.

- **The fruiting body** grows overnight after rain and lasts just a few days. The mycelium may survive underground for many years.

- **The fruiting body** is covered by a protective cap. On the underside of the cap are lots of thin sheets called gills which are covered in spores.

- **A mushroom's** gills can produce 16 billion spores in its brief lifetime.

- **The biggest mushrooms** have caps up to 50 cm across and grow up to 40 cm tall.

- **Fairy rings** are rings of bright green grass once said to have been made by fairies dancing. They are actually made by a mushroom as its hyphae spread outwards. Chemicals they release make grass grow greener. Gradually the mycelium at the centre dies while outer edges grow and the ring gets bigger.

Forestry

▲ The signs of pollarding are easy to see in these trees in winter when the leaves are gone.

- **Forests** provide fuel, timber, paper, resins, varnishes, dyes, rubber, kapok and much more besides.

- **Softwood** is timber from coniferous trees such as pine, larch, fir and spruce. 75–80 percent of the natural forests of northern Asia, Europe and the USA are softwood.

★ STAR FACT ★
Every year the world uses three billion cubic metres of wood – a pile as big as a football stadium and as high as Mt Everest.

- **In vast plantations** fast-growing conifers are set in straight rows so they are easy to cut down.

- **Hardwood** is timber from broad-leaved trees such as oak. Most hardwood forests are in the tropics.

- **Hardwood trees** take over a century to reach maturity.

- **Tropical hardwoods** such as mahogany are becoming rare as more hardwood is cut for timber.

- **Pollarding** is cutting the topmost branches of a tree so new shoots grow from the trunk to the same length.

- **Coppicing** is cutting tree stems at ground level to encourage several stems to grow from the same root.

- **Half the world's remaining** rainforests will be gone by 2020 if they are cut down at today's rate.

Sugar

- **Sugars** are sweet-tasting natural substances made by plants and animals. All green plants make sugar.

- **Fruit and honey** contain a sugar called fructose. Milk contains the sugar lactose.

- ▼▶ *Crystals of demerara sugar are made from the sugary juice from the stems of the tropical sugar cane.*

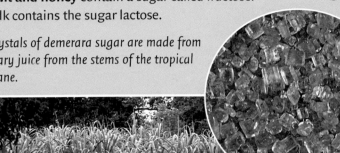

- **The most common sugar** is called sucrose, or just sugar – like the sugar you sprinkle on cereal.

- **Sugar is made** from sugar cane and sugar beet.

- **Sugar cane** is a tropical grass with woody stems 2–5 m tall. It grows in places like India and Brazil.

- **Sugar juice is made** from cane by shredding and crushing the stems and soaking them in hot water to dissolve the sugar.

- **Sugar beet** is a turnip-like plant that grows in temperate countries.

- **Sugar juice is made** from beet by soaking thin slices of the root in hot water to dissolve the sugar.

- **Sugar juice** is warmed to evaporate water so crystals form.

- **White sugar** is sugar made from sugar beet, or by refining (purifying) cane-sugar. Brown sugars such as muscovado and demerara are unrefined cane-sugar. Molasses and black treacle are by-products of cane-sugar refining.

Leaves

- **Leaves** are a plant's powerhouse, using sunlight to join water and carbon dioxide to make sugar, the plant's fuel.

- **Leaves are** broad and flat to catch maximum sunlight.

- **Leaves** are joined to the stem by a stalk called a petiole.

- **The flat part** of the leaf is called the blade.

- **The leaf blade** is like a sandwich with two layers of cells holding a thick filling of green cells.

- **The green** comes from the chemical chlorophyll. It is this that catches sunlight to make sugar in photosynthesis.

- **Chlorophyll** is held in tiny bags in each cell called chloroplasts.

- **A network** of branching veins (tubes) supplies the leaf with water. It also transports the sugar made there to the rest of the plant.

- **Air containing** carbon dioxide is drawn into the leaf through pores on the underside called stomata. Stomata also let out water in a process called transpiration.

- **To cut down water loss** in dry places, leaves may be rolled-up, long and needle-like, or covered in hairs or wax. Climbing plants, such as peas, have leaf tips that coil into stalks called tendrils to help the plant cling.

▶ *A hugely magnified slice through a leaf, showing the cells and veins.*

Leaf veins containing tiny tubes

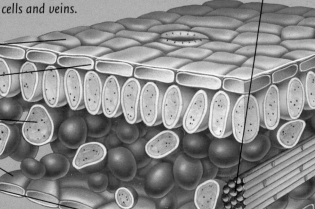

Waterproof wax coat

Upper skin of leaf

Green cells

Lower skin of leaf

Leaf pores (stomata)

Rotting trees

- **Trees** are dying in forests all the time.
- **In the past** foresters used to clear away dead trees or chop down those that were dying, but it is now clear that they play a vital part in the woodland ecosystem.
- **When a tree falls** it crashes down through the leaves and opens up a patch of woodland, called a glade, to the sky.
- **In the glade** saplings (new young trees) can sprout and flourish in the sunlight.
- **Many other woodland plants** flourish in the sunshine of a glade.
- **Flowers** such as foxgloves and rosebay willowherbs often spring up in a glade.

- **Bracken and shrubs** such as brambles grow quickly in a glade.
- **The rotting tree trunk** provides food for fungi such as green-staining and candle snuff fungus.
- **Many insects** such as beetles find a home in the rotting wood.
- **As the rotting tree is broken down** it not only provides food for plants, insects and bacteria, it enriches the soil too.

◀ Rotting trees provide a home for many kinds of plants, such as these tiny green liverworts, growing on an old stump.

Tulips

▲ Huge numbers of tulips are now grown in the fields in Holland.

- **Tulips** are flowers that bloom in spring from bulbs.
- **Tulips are** monocots and produce one large, bell-shaped bloom at the end of each stem.
- **There are about** 100 species of wild tulip, growing right across Asia to China.

- **Tulips** come in most colours but blue. Reds and yellows are common, but they vary from white to deep purple.
- **There are over 4000** garden varieties.
- **Most tulips** are 'late bloomers' with names like breeders, cottages and parrots.
- **Mid-season bloomers** include Mendels and Darwins.
- **Early season** bloomers include single-flowereds and double-flowered earlies.
- **Tulips** were introduced to Europe in 1551 by the Viennese ambassador to Turkey, Augier de Busbecq. But Holland became the centre of tulip-growing early in the 1600s, when Europe was gripped by 'tulipmania'. At this time, people would exchange mansions for a single tulip bulb. Holland is still the centre of tulip growing.

> ★ STAR FACT ★
> The word *tulip* comes from the Turkish for 'turban', because of their shape.

Herbs

- **Herbs** are small plants used as medicines or to flavour food.

- **Most herbs** are perennial and have soft stems that die back in winter.

- **With some herbs,** such as rosemary, only the leaves are used. With others, such as garlic, the bulb is used. Fennel is used for its seeds as well as its bulb and leaves. Coriander is used for its leaves and seeds.

- **Basil** gets its name from the Greek *basilikon* or 'kingly', because it was so highly valued around the Mediterranean for its strong flavour. In the Middle Ages, judges and officials used to carry it in posies to ward off unpleasant smells.

- **Rosemary** is a coastal plant and gets its name from the Latin *ros marinus*, meaning 'sea dew'. Herbalists once thought that it improved memory.

- **Bay leaves** are the leaves of a laurel tree. They were used to make crowns for athletes, heroes and poets in ancient Rome. It is said that a bay tree planted by your house protects it from lightning.

- **Oregano**, or marjoram, is a Mediterranean herb used in Italian cooking. The plant gave its name to the American state of Oregon where it is now very common.

- **Sage** is a herb thought by herbalists of old to have special healing qualities. Its scientific name *Salvia* comes from the Latin word *salvere*, 'to save'.

- **St John's wort** is a perennial herb with yellow flowers, which was said to have healing qualities given by St John the Baptist. The red juice of its leaves represented his blood. Now many people use it to treat depression.

▶ These are just some of the more common herbs used in cooking, either fresh or dried. The flavour comes from what are called 'essential oils' in the leaves.

> ★ STAR FACT ★
> The root of the mandrake was supposed to have magical properties. Anyone who uprooted one was said to die, so people tied the root to a dog's tail to pull it up.

Thyme

Rosemary

Mint

Dill

Parsley

Bay

Fennel

Sage

Chives

Monocotyledons

- **Monocotyledons** are one of the two basic classes of flowering plant. The other is dicotyledons.
- **Monocotyledons** are plants that sprout a single leaf from their seeds.
- **Monocotyledons** are also known as monocots or Liliopsida.
- **There are about** 50,000 species of monocots – about a quarter of all flowering plants.
- **Monocots** include grasses, cereals, bamboos, date palms, aloes, snake plants, tulips, orchids and daffodils.
- **Monocots** tend to grow quickly and their stems stay soft and pliable, except for bamboos and palms. Most are herbaceous.

▲ Daffodils are typical monocots, with long lance-like leaves and petals in threes.

- **The tubes or veins** in monocot leaves run parallel to each other. They also develop a thick tangle of thin roots rather than a single long 'tap' root, like dicots.
- **The flower parts of monocots** such as petals tend to be set in threes or multiples of three.
- **Unlike dicots**, monocot stems grow from the inside. Dicots have a cambium, which is the layer of growing cells near the outside of the stem. Monocots rarely have a cambium.
- **Monocots** are thought to have appeared about 90 million years ago, developing from water lily-like dicots living in swamps and rivers.

Medicinal plants

▲ Aspirin is the painkiller most widely used today. It first came from the bark of willow trees.

- **Prehistoric neanderthal people** probably used plants as medicines at least 50,000 years ago.
- **Until quite recently** herbaceous plants were our main source of medicines. Plants used as medicines were listed in books called herbals.

- **An ancient Chinese** list of 1892 herbal remedies drawn up over 3000 years ago is still used today.
- **The famous illustrated herbal** of Greek physician Dioscorides was made in the 1st century BC.
- **The most famous English** herbalist was Nicholas Culpeper, who wrote A Physical Directory in 1649.
- **Most medicines,** except antibiotics, come from flowering plants or were first found in flowering plants.
- **Powerful painkilling** drugs come from the seeds of the opium poppy.
- **Digitalis** is a heart drug that came from foxgloves. It is poisonous in large doses.
- **Garlic** is thought to protect the body against heart disease.

★ STAR FACT ★
Vincristine is a drug made from the Madagascar periwinkle that helps children to fight cancer.

Pine trees

- **Pine trees** are evergreen conifers with long needle-like leaves. They grow mostly in sandy or rocky soils in cool places.

- **Pines** are the largest family of conifers.

- **There 90–100 species of pine** – most of them coming originally from northern Eurasia and North America.

- **Pines grow** fast and straight, reaching their full height in less than 20 years – which is why they provide 75 percent of the world's timber.

- **Some pines** produce a liquid called resin which is used to make turpentine, paint and soap.

- **Soft or white pines**, such as sugar pines and piñons, have soft wood. They grow needles in bundles of five and have little resin.

- **Hard or yellow pines**, such as Scots, Corsican and loblolly pines, have harder wood. They grow needles in bundles of two or three and make lots of resin.

◀ Like all conifers, Corsican pines produce cones. The cones look very different from flowers but serve the same purpose – making the seeds from which new trees grow.

- **Eurasian pines** include the Scots pine, Corsican pine, black pine, pinaster and stone pine.

- **North American pines** include the eastern white pine, sugar pine, stone pines, piñons, Ponderosa pine, and Monterey pine.

- **The sugar pine** is the biggest of all pines, often growing up to 70 m tall and 3.5 m thick. The eastern white pine has valuable fine white wood.

Tropical fruit

- **Tropical fruits** grow mainly in the tropics where it is warm because they cannot survive even a light frost.

- **The best-known tropical fruits** are bananas and pineapples. Others include guavas, breadfruit, lychees, melons, mangoes and papayas.

- **Banana plants** are gigantic herbs with trunks that grow 3–6 m high.

- **Alexander the Great** saw bananas in India in 326BC. Bananas were taken to the Caribbean from the Canaries c. 1550. They are now one of the main Caribbean crops.

- **There are hundreds** of varieties of banana. Most widely used is the Gros Michel. Plantains are cooking bananas.

- **Pineapples** come from Central America, and were seen by Columbus and Sir Walter Raleigh.

- **The Portuguese** took pineapples to India about 1550. Thailand is now the world's leading producer.

- **Mangoes** grow on evergreen trees of the cashew family in Burma and India.

- **The mango** is sacred to Buddhists because the mango groves provided welcome shade for Buddha.

- **Melons** are a huge group of big, round fruit with soft, juicy flesh, including canteloupes. They grow on trailing vines. Watermelons are not true melons.

▼ Bananas are picked green and unripe, shipped in refrigerated ships, then artificially ripened with 'ethylene' gas to turn them yellow.

Tropical rainforest

Tall, isolated trees called
emergents grow up to 60m tall

Main canopy of
broad-leaved
evergreen trees

Plants called
epiphytes grow
on the branches
of trees

Climbing
lianas

- **Tropical rainforests** are warm and wet, with over 2000 mm of rain a year and average temperatures over 20°C. They are the world's richest plant habitats.

- **Flowering plants** (angiosperms) originated in tropical rainforests. Eleven of the 13 oldest families live here.

- **Most rainforest trees** are broad-leaved and evergreen.

- **Trees** of the Amazon rainforest include rosewood, Brazil nut and rubber, plus myrtle, laurel and palms. Trees in the African rainforest include mahogany, ebony, limba, wenge, agba, iroko and sapele.

> ★ STAR FACT ★
> One 23 hectare area of Malaysian rainforest
> has 375 species of tree with trunks
> thicker than 91 cm.

- **Many rainforest plants** have big, bright flowers to attract birds and insects in the gloom. Flowers pollinated by birds are often red, those by night-flying moths white or pink and those by day-flying insects yellow or orange.

- **The gloom** means many plants need big seeds to store enough food while they grow. So they grow fragrant fruits that attract animals to eat the fruit and spread the seed in their body waste. Fruit bats are drawn to mangoes. Orang-utans and tigers eat durians.

- **Many trees** grow flowers on their trunks to make them easy for animals to reach. This is called cauliflory.

- **Rainforest trees** are covered with epiphytes – plants whose roots never reach the soil but take water from the air.

- **Many plants are parasitic** including mistletoes and rafflesia. They feed on other plants.

Dense understorey of shrubs

◀ Most tropical rainforests have several layers. Towering above the main forest are isolated emergent trees up to 60 m tall. Below these, 30–50 m above the ground, is a dense canopy of leaves and branches at the top of tall, straight trees. In the gloom beneath is the understorey where young emergents, small conical trees and a huge range of shrubs grow. Clinging lianas wind their way up through the trees and epiphytes grow high on tree branches and trunks where they can reach daylight.

The first crops

> ★ STAR FACT ★
> Beans, bottle gourds and water chestnuts were
> grown at Spirit Cave in Thailand 11,000 years ago.

- **The first crops** were probably root crops like turnips. Grains and green vegetables were probably first grown as crops later.

- **Einkorn and emmer** wheat and wild barley may have been cultivated by Natufians (stone-age people) about 7000BC at Ali Kosh on the Iran-Iraq border.

- **Pumpkins** and beans were cultivated in Mexico c.7000BC.

- **People** in the Amazon have grown manioc to make a flat bread called *cazabi* for thousands of years.

- **Corn** was probably first grown about 9000 years ago from the teosinte plant of the Mexican highlands.

- **Russian botanist** N. I. Vavilov worked out that wheat and rye came from the wild grasses of central Asia, millet and barley from highland China and rice from India.

- **Millet** was grown in China from c.4500BC.

- **In N. Europe** the first grains were those now called fat hen, gold of pleasure and curl-topped lady's thumb.

- **Sumerian** farmers in the Middle East c.3000BC grew barley along with wheat, flax, dates, apples, plums and grapes.

▲ *Emmer wheat is one of the oldest of all cereal crops. It was probably first sown deliberately from wild grass seeds about 10,000 years ago.*

Magnolia

▲ *Magnolias have a single large typically white or pink flower at the end of each stem. This is the evergreen Magnolia kobus.*

- **Magnolias** are evergreen shrubs, climbers and trees.

- **Magnolias** are named after the French botanist Pierre Magnol (1638–1715).

- **They produce** beautiful large white or pink flowers and are popular garden plants.

- **Nutmegs, custard apples,** ylang-ylangs and tulip trees are all kinds of magnolia.

- **There are** over 80 different kinds of magnolia.

- **Magnolias may be** the most ancient of all flowering plants. Their fossil remains have been found in rocks 120 million years old – when the dinosaurs lived.

- **A seed 2,000 years old,** found by archaeologists (people who study ancient remains) in Japan was planted in 1982. It grew and produced an unusual flower with eight petals.

- **The most popular** garden magnolia was bred in a garden near Paris, France, from a wild Japanese kind (*Magnolia liliiflora*) and a wild Chinese kind (*Magnolia denudata*).

- **Magnolia trees** have the largest leaves and flowers of any tree outside the tropical forests.

- **The cucumber tree** –a kind of magnolia – is named after its seed clusters, which look like cucumbers.

Tundra

▲ In spring the tundra bursts into glorious colour as flowers bloom to take advantage of the brief warm weather.

- **Tundras** are regions so cold and with so little rain that tall trees cannot grow.

- **Tundras** are typically covered in snow for at least half the year. Even in summer the soil 1 m or so below the ground may be permanently frozen.

- **The frozen ground** stops water draining away and makes tundras marshy and damp.

- **Winter temperatures** in the tundra can drop to -40°C. Even summer temperatures are rarely above 12°C on average.

- **Mosses and lichens**, grasses and sedges, heathers and low shrubs grow in tundra. Trees only grow in stunted forms such as dwarf willows and ash trees.

- **In spring** tundra plants grow quickly and bright wildflowers spread across the ground.

- **Arctic tundras** occur in places like northern Siberia and Canada.

- **Alpine tundras** occur high on mountains everywhere.

- **Arctic flowers** include saxifrages, Arctic poppies, fireweeds, cinquefoil, louseworts and stonecrops.

- **Alpine flowers** are often the same as Arctic flowers. They include mountain avens, gentians, saxifrages and snowbells.

Coffee and tea

- **Coffee** comes from the glossy, evergreen *Coffee arabica* shrub which originally grew wild in Ethiopia. Coffee is now grown in tropical countries around the world.

- **The coffee plant** is a mountain plant and grows best from about 1000 to 2500 m up.

- **Coffee beans** are not actually beans at all; they are the seeds inside red berries.

- **Coffee plants** can grow over 6 m tall, but they are usually pruned to under 4 m to make picking easier.

- **A coffee plant** yields only enough berries to make about 0.7 kg of coffee each year.

- **Coffee berries** are picked by hand then pulped to remove the flesh and finally roasted.

▲ Coffee berries appear green at first, then turn yellow and eventually bright red as they ripen.

> ★ STAR FACT ★
> Legend says Ethiopian goatherds discovered coffee when they saw their goats staying awake all night after eating the berries of the coffee plant.

- **Tea** is the leaves of the evergreen tea plant that grows in the tropics, mostly between 1000 and 2000 m.

- **Tea plants** have small, white, scented flowers and nuts that look like hazelnuts.

- **Tea plants** grow 9 m tall but they are pruned to 3 m.

Maple trees

- **Maples** are a huge group of trees belonging to the Acer family.

- **Maples grow** all over the temperate regions of the northern hemisphere, but especially in China.

- **Many maple tree leaves** turn brilliant shades of red in autumn.

◀ *All maple trees have winged seeds called samaras or keys. Many also have three-lobed leaves, like these of the sugar maple.*

- **Several North American maple trees,** including the sugar maple and the black maple, give maple syrup.

- **Maple syrup** is 'sweet-water' sap. This is different from ordinary sap and flows from wounds during times of thaws when the tree is not growing. Syrup is collected between mid January and mid April.

- **Maple syrup** was used by the Native Americans of the Great Lakes and St Lawrence River regions long before Europeans arrived in North America.

- **About 30 litres** of sap give 1 litre of maple syrup.

- **The leaf of the sugar maple tree** is Canada's national symbol.

- **Many small maples** are grown as garden plants. Japanese maples have been carefully bred over the centuries to give all kinds of varieties with different leaf shapes and colours.

- **The red maple** is planted in many North American cities for its brilliant red autumn leaves.

Wildflowers

- **All flowers** were originally wild. Garden flowers have been bred over the centuries to be very different from their wild originals.

- **Wildflowers** are flowers that have developed naturally.

- **Most wildflowers** are smaller and more delicate than their garden cousins.

- **Each** kind of place has its own special range of wildflowers, although many wildflowers have now been spread to different places by humans.

- **Heathlands** may have purple blooms of heathers, yellow gorse and scarlet pimpernel.

- **In meadow grass** flowers like buttercups, daisies, clover, forget-me-nots and ragged robin often grow.

- **In deciduous woodlands** flowers like bluebells, primroses, daffodils and celandines grow.

- **By the sea** among the rocks, sea campion and pink thrift may bloom, while up on the cliffs, there may be birdsfoot trefoil among the grasses.

- **As humans** take over larger and larger areas of the world, and as farmers use more and more weedkillers on the land, many wildflowers are becoming very rare. Some are so rare that they are protected by law.

- **The lady's slipper orchid** grows in parts of Europe, Asia and America, usually in moist, woodland areas.

▶ *There are now very few meadows with rich displays of wildflowers like this.*

Arctic plants

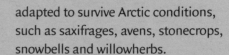

- **The Arctic circle** is icy cold and dark for nine months of the year, but for a few months in summer it is daylight almost all the time.

- **Over 900 species** of plants cope with the Arctic climate.

- **Full-size trees** are rare in the Arctic; but grasses and sedges, mosses and lichens are common.

- **Willow trees** grow in the Arctic, but because of the cold and fierce wind, they grow less than 10 cm tall, spreading out along the ground instead.

- **Many Arctic** plants are evergreen so they are ready to make the most of the brief summer.

- **Many small** flowers are specially

adapted to survive Arctic conditions, such as saxifrages, avens, stonecrops, snowbells and willowherbs.

- **The Arctic poppy** is the flower that blooms nearest the North Pole.

- **Butterflies and bees** are rare in the Arctic, so many plants, like mustard, rely on the wind for pollination.

- **The soil is so poor** in the Arctic that seeds make the most of any animal corpse, such as that of a musk ox. Arctic flowers often spring up inside skulls and near bones.

- **Some plants** have dark leaves and stems to soak up the sun's warmth quickly and so melt the snow.

◀ In summer, the Arctic bursts into brief life with tiny flowers and ground berries like bilberries.

Pollination

- **For seeds** to develop, pollen from a flower's male anther must get to a female stigma.

- **Some flowers are** self-pollinating and the pollen moves from an anther to a stigma on the same plant.

- **In cross-pollinating** flowers, the pollen from the anthers must be carried to a stigma on a different plant of the same kind.

- **Some pollen** is carried by the wind.

- **Most pollen** is carried on the bodies of insects such as bees or by birds or bats that visit the flower.

- **Insect-pollinated flowers** are often brightly coloured and sweet-smelling to attract bees and butterflies.

◀ Many flowers rely on attracting bees to carry their pollen.

- **Bees and butterflies** are also drawn by the flower's sweet juice or nectar. As they sip the nectar, they may brush pollen on to the stigma, or take some on their bodies from anthers to the stigma of other flowers.

- **Bees and butterflies** are drawn to blue, yellow and pink flowers. White flowers draw night-flying moths.

- **Many flowers** have honey guides – markings to guide the bees in. These are often invisible to us and can only be seen in ultraviolet light, which bees can see.

- **The cuckoopint** smells like cow-dung to attract the flies that carry its pollen.

The farming year

A few days after the harvest the soil is cultivated to get rid of unwanted weeds

Harvest time in late summer when the wheat is harvested

After cultivation, the soil is prepared by ploughing and harrowing

About six weeks after the harvest, the seeds are sown in the prepared soil

▶ This illustration shows the typical sequence of events in a grain farmer's year, from ploughing and sowing the seed right through to harvest the following autumn.

The seeds sprout before winter sets in, but don't begin to ripen until the following spring

- **The farming year** varies considerably around the world, and farmers do different tasks at different times of year in different places.

- **In temperate regions** the crop farmer's year starts in autumn after the harvest. Once the straw has been baled and the surplus burned, the race starts to prepare the soil for next year's crops before snow and frost set in.

◀ Without artificial fertilizers, the soil is quickly exhausted if grain crops are planted year after year. So in the past, farmers rotated fields with different crops to allow the soil to rest. Rotation systems varied, but usually included grain, green plants, and 'rest' crops. The earliest systems had just two alternating fields. Medieval farmers used three fields. From the 1700s, rotations became more complex.

- **A tractor** drags a cultivator (like a large rake) across the field to make weeds 'chit' (germinate). A few days later the soil is cultivated again to uproot the seedlings.

- **Next the soil** is ploughed to break up the soil ready for the seed to be sown, then harrowed to smooth out the deep furrows made by the plough.

- **Within six weeks** of the harvest if the weather holds, winter wheat or barley seed is sown, fertilizer is applied and the seed soon sprouts like a carpet of grass.

- **In winter,** the farmer turns to tasks like hedge-cutting, ditching and fencing.

- **In spring** potatoes, oats and spring wheat and barley are planted, and winter crops treated with nitrogen fertilizer. In spring and summer, many farmers treat crops with 30 or more pesticides and weedkillers.

- **As the summer wears on** the wheat turns gold and is ready for harvesting when the electronic moisture metre shows it contains less than 18 percent moisture.

- **If the summer** is damp, the grain's moisture content may not go below 25 percent, making harvesting difficult. But warm sun can quickly rectify the situation.

- **The farming year** ends with the harvest. In the past this used to be separated into various stages – harvesting, threshing, winnowing and baling. Now combine harvesters allow the farmer to complete them all at one go.

Boreal forest

- **Forests in cool regions** in the north of Asia and North America, bordering on the Arctic circle, are called boreal forests. The word *boreal* means 'northern'.

- **Winters** in boreal regions are long and cold. Days are short and snow lies permanently on the ground.

- **In Russia and Siberia** boreal forest is called *taiga*, which is Russian for 'little sticks'.

- **Boreal forests** are mostly evergreen conifers such as pine – especially Scots pine – spruce, larch and fir.

- **In Europe** boreal forests include Norway spruce and Sukaczev larch. In Siberia, there are trees such as Siberian larch and fir, chosenia and Siberian stone pine.

- **North American** forests include balsam firs, black spruces, jack pines and lodgepole pines.

▶ Boreal forests cover 17 percent of the Earth's land area. For nine months of the year they are cold and dark, but they spring to life in the three-month summer.

- **Boreal forest floors** are covered with carpets of needles. Twinflowers, calypso orchids, lingonberries, baneberries, and coral roots are among the few plants that will grow.

- **Boreal forest trees** are good at recovering after fire. Indeed jack pine and black spruce cones only open to release their seeds after a fire.

- **The Black Dragon Fire** of 1987 in the boreal forests of China and Russia was the biggest fire in history.

> ★ STAR FACT ★
> Half the ground under conifers is covered in moss and lichen.

The Green Revolution

- **Since ancient times** farmers have tried to improve crops. They brushed pollen from one species on to another to gain desirable qualities in the next generation of plants.

- **In 1876** Charles Darwin discovered that inbreeding – pollinating with almost identical plants – made plants less vigorous. Cross-breeding between different strains produced healthier plants.

- **In the early 1900s** American scientists found that they could improve the protein content of corn by inbreeding – but the yield was poor.

- **In 1917** Donald Jones discovered the 'double-cross', combining four strains (not the normal two) to create a hybrid corn giving high yield and high protein.

▶ Forty years ago, many farmers abandoned traditional wheat seeds and began planting big 'superwheat' seeds.

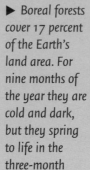

- **Hybrid corn** changed US farming, raising yields from 2000 litres per hectare in 1933 to 7220 in 1980.

- **In the 1960s** US farmers began growing wheat crosses such as Gaines, developed by Norman Borlaug from Japanese dwarf wheats.

- **Gaines and Nugaines** are short-stemmed wheats that grow fast and give huge yields – but they need masses of artificial fertilizers and pesticides.

- **In India and Asia** new dwarf wheats and rices created a 'Green Revolution', doubling yields in the 1960s and 1970s.

- **The Green Revolution** means farmers now use ten times as much nitrogen fertilizer as in 1960.

- **The huge cost** of special seeds, fertilizers and pesticides has often meant that only big agribusinesses can keep up, forcing small farmers out of business.

Mosses

- **Mosses** are tiny, green, non-flowering plants found throughout the world. They form cushions just a few millimetres thick on walls, rocks and logs.

- **Unlike other plants** they have no true roots. Instead, they take in moisture from the air through their stems and tiny, root-like threads called rhizoids.

- **Mosses reproduce** from minute spores in two stages.

- **First tadpole-like** male sex cells are made on bag-like stems called antheridae and swim to join the female eggs on cup-like stems called archegonia.

- **Then a stalk** called a sporophyte grows from the ova. On top is a capsule holding thousands of spores.

- **When the time** is right, the sporophyte capsule bursts, ejecting spores. If spores land in a suitable place, male and female stems grow and the process begins again.

- **Mosses** can survive for weeks without water, then soak it up like a sponge when it rains.

▶ Mosses grow on rocks in damp places everywhere. They take in the moisture they need to grow from the air, but to reproduce, they need to be completely soaked.

- **The sphagnum or peat moss** can soak up 25 times its own weight of water.

- **Male cells** can only swim to female cells if the moss is partly under water. So mosses often grow near streams where they get splashed.

- **Spanish moss** was often used as a filler in packing cases and to pad upholstery.

Rhododendrons

- **Rhododendrons** are a big group of 800 different trees and shrubs that belong to the heath family.

- **The word 'rhododendron'** means 'rose tree'.

- **Most rhododendrons** came originally from the Himalayas and the mountains of Malaysia where they form dense thickets.

- **Many rhododendrons** are now widely cultivated for their big red or white blooms and evergreen leaves.

- **There are over 6000** different cultivated varieties of rhododendron.

- **The spectacular June blooming** of the catawba rhododendron or mountain rosebay in the Great Smoky Mountains, USA, is now a tourist attraction.

- **The Dahurian** is a famous purply pink rhododendron from Siberia and Mongolia.

- **The Smirnow** was discovered in the 1880s high up in the Caucasus Mts on the Georgian–Turkish border.

- **Smirnows** have been bred with other rhododendrons to make them very hardy.

- **Azaleas** were once considered a separate group of plants, but they are now classified with rhododendrons.

◀ Rhododendrons have thrived so well in places where they have been introduced that many people now consider them weeds.

Carnivorous plants

- **Plants that trap** insects for food are called carnivorous plants. They live in places where they cannot get enough nitrogen from the soil and so the insects provide the nitrogen.

- **There are 550 species** living in places from the high peaks of New Zealand to the swamps of Carolina.

- **The butterwort** gets its name because its leaves ooze drops that make them glisten like butter. These drops contains the plant's digestive juices.

◄ Pitchers hang on long tendrils that grow high into the branches of tropical rainforests. Some pitchers are tiny and can trap nothing bigger than an ant. The pitchers of the Nepenthes rajah are big enough for a rat.

- **The sundew** can tell the difference between flesh and other substances and only reacts to flesh.

- **The sundew's** leaves are covered in tentacles that ooze a sticky substance called mucilage.

- **The sundew** wraps up its victims in its tentacles and suffocates them in slime in under ten seconds.

- **A Venus fly-trap's** trap will only shut if touched at least twice in 20 seconds.

- **Insects** are lured on to many carnivorous plants by sweet-tasting nectar – or the smell of rotting meat.

- **The juice** of a pitcher plant will dissolve a chunk of steak to nothing in a few days.

- **The bladders** of bladderworts were once thought to be air sacs to keep the plant afloat. In fact, they are tiny traps for water insects.

◄ Insects are lured into the jaw-like leaf trap of the Venus fly-trap with nectar. Once the insect lands, the jaws clamp shut on the victim in a fraction of a second. At once the plant secretes juices that drown, then dissolve, the insect.

The fly touches hairs that send an electrical signal to cells on the side of the trap

▼ Like the Venus fly-trap, the Sarracenia is a native of North America. But instead of actively capturing its prey, it provides a deep tube for them to fall into. Insects drawn to the nectar round its rim slide in and are unable to climb out.

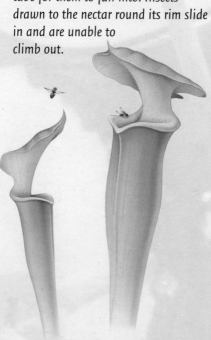

When triggered, cells on the outside of the trap expand instantly and cells on the inside contract, pulling the trap shut

Tentacles covered in drops of sticky mucilage

◄ When an insect lands on the sticky tentacles of a sundew, it struggles to free itself – but this struggling stimulates the tentacles to tighten their grip. Soon the tentacles exude a digestive juice that dissolves the victim.

Temperate fruit

- **Fruits of temperate regions** must have a cool winter to grow properly.

- **The main temperate fruits** are apples, pears, plums, apricots, peaches, grapes and cherries.

- **Apples were eaten** by the earliest Europeans hundreds of thousands of years ago. They were spread through the USA by Indians, trappers and travellers like Johnny 'Appleseed' Chapman.

- **The world** picks 32 million tonnes of apples a year, half are eaten fresh and a quarter are made into the alcoholic drink cider. The USA is the world's leading producer of cider apples.

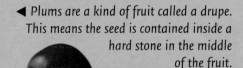

◀ *Plums are a kind of fruit called a drupe. This means the seed is contained inside a hard stone in the middle of the fruit.*

◀ *Pears are the second most important temperate fruit after apples. The leading producer is China.*

- **The world's most** popular pear is the Williams' Bon Chrétien or Bartlett. The best is said to to be the Doyenné du Comice, first grown in France in 1849.

- **New pear trees** are grown not from seeds but by grafting branches on to roots such as those of quinces.

- **Plums** came originally from the Caucasus Mountains in Turkey and Turkey is still the world's major plum grower. The damson plum came from Damascus.

- **Plums** are dried to make prunes.

- **The peach** is 87 percent water and has far fewer calories than fruit like apples and pears.

- **Grapes are grown** in vineyards to make wine. Grape-growing or viticulture is described in detail in Ancient Egyptian hieroglyphs of 2400 BC.

Evergreen trees

- **An evergreen** is a plant that keeps its leaves in winter.

- **Many tropical broad-leaved trees** are evergreen.

- **In cool temperate regions** and the Arctic, most evergreen trees are conifers such as pines and firs. They have needle-like leaves.

- **Old needles** do turn yellow and drop, but they are replaced by new needles (unless the tree is unhealthy).

- **Evergreens** may suffer from sunscald – too much sun – in dry, sunny spots, especially in early spring.

- **Five coniferous groups**, including larches and cypresses, are not evergreen.

- **Many evergreens** were sacred to ancient cultures. The laurel or bay was sacred to the Greek god Apollo and used by the Romans as a symbol of high achievement.

- **Yews are grown** in many European churchyards – perhaps because the trees were planted on the sites by pagans in the days before Christianity. But the bark of the yew tree and its seeds are poisonous.

- **The sakaki** is sacred to the Japanese Shinto religion, and entire trees are uprooted to appear in processions.

▼ *In cool northern climates where the summers are brief, conifers stay evergreen to make the most of the available sunshine.*

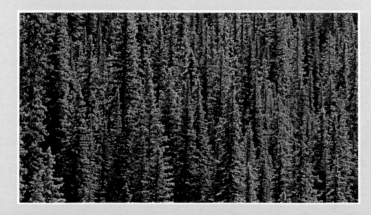

Fertilizers

▲ Once the soil is broken up by ploughing, fertilizers are applied to prepare the soil for planting.

- **Fertilizers** are natural or artificial substances added to soil to make crops and garden plants grow better.

- **Natural fertilizers** such as manure and compost have been used since the earliest days of farming.

- **Manure** comes mostly from farm animals, though in some countries, human waste is used.

- **Manure** has the chemicals nitrogen, phosphorus and potassium plants need for growth. It is also rich in humus, organic matter that helps keep water in the soil.

- **Artificial fertilizers** are usually liquid or powdered chemicals (or occasionally gas), containing a mix of nitrogen, phosphorus or potassium. They also have traces of sulphur, magnesium and calcium.

- **Nitrogen fertilizers**, also called nitrate fertilisers, are made from ammonia, which is made from natural gas.

- **The first fertilizer** factory was set up by Sir John Lawes in Britain in 1843. He made superphosphate by dissolving bones in acid. Phosphates now come from bones or rocks.

- **Potassium fertilizers** come from potash dug up in mines.

- **The use of artificial** fertilizers has increased in the last 40 years, especially in the developed world.

- **Environmentalists** worry about the effects of nitrate fertilizers entering water supplies, and the huge amount of energy needed to make, transport and apply them.

Flower facts

- **The world's tallest** flower is the 2.5 m Titan arum which grows in the tropical jungles of Sumatra.

- **The Titan arum** is shaped so that flies are trapped in a chamber at the bottom.

- **The world's biggest flower** is Rafflesia, which grows in the jungles of Borneo and Sumatra. It is 1 m in diameter and weighs up to 11 kg.

- **Rafflesia** is a parasite and has no leaves, root or stems.

- **Rafflesia** and the Titan arum both smell like rotting meat to attract the insects that pollinate them.

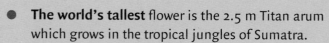

▶ Rafflesia was 'discovered' by British explorer John Arnold in 1818 and named by him after the famous British colonialist Stamford Raffles.

- **The world's smallest flower** is the Wolffia duckweed of Australia. This is a floating water plant less than 0.6 mm across. It can only be seen clearly under a magnifying glass.

- **The biggest flowerhead** is the *Puya raimondii* bromeliad of Bolivia which can be up to 2.5 m across and 10 m tall and have 8000 individual blooms.

- **The Puya raimondii** takes 150 years to grow its first flower, then dies.

- **Two Australian orchids** bloom underground. No-one knows how they pollinate.

- **Stapelia flowers** not only smell like rotting meat to attract the flies that pollinate them – they look like it too (all pinky-brown and wrinkled).

Fruit

▶ There are three kinds of cherries – sweet, sour, and 'dukes', which are sweet-sour cross. We eat mainly sweet cherries like these.

- **Scientists** say a fruit is the ovary of a plant after the eggs are pollinated and grow into seeds. Corn grains, cucumbers, bean pods and acorns are fruit as well as apples and so on.

- **Some fruits**, such as oranges, are soft and juicy. The hard pips are the seeds.

- **With some fruits** such as hazelnuts and almonds, the flesh turns to a hard dry shell.

- **Fleshy fruits** are either berries like oranges which are all flesh, aggregate fruits like blackberries which are made from lots of berries from a single flower or multiple fruits like pineapples, which are single fruits made from an entire multiple flowerhead.

- **Legumes** such as peas and beans are soft, dry fruits held in a case called a pod.

- **Berries** and other juicy fruits are called 'true fruits' because they are made from the ovary of the flower alone.

- **Apples and pears** are called 'false fruits' because they include parts other than the flower's ovary.

- **In an apple** only the core is the ovary.

- **Drupes** are fruit like plums, mangoes and cherries with no pips but just a hard stone in the centre containing the seeds. Aggregate fruits like raspberries are clusters of drupes.

- **Walnuts and dogwood** are actually drupes like cherries.

Roots

- **Roots are** the parts of a plant that grow down into soil or water, anchoring it and soaking up all the water and minerals the plant needs to grow.

- **In some plants** such as beetroots, the roots are also a food store.

- **When a seed** begins to grow, its first root is called a primary root. This branches into secondary roots.

> ★ STAR FACT ★
> The roots of the South African wild fig tree can grow 120 m down into the ground.

- **Roots** are protected at the end by a thimble-shaped root cap as they probe through the soil.

- **On every root** there are tiny root hairs that help it take up water and minerals.

- **Some plants,** such as carrots, have a single large root, called a taproot, with just a few fine roots branching off.

- **Some plants** such as grass have lots of small roots, called fibrous roots, branching off in all directions.

- **Some kinds of orchid** that live on trees have 'aerial' roots that cling to the branches.

- **Mistletoe** has roots that penetrate its host tree.

◀ A tree blown over in a gale reveals some of the dense mat of roots it needs to get enough water and nutrients.

Harvesting grain

- **When grain** is ripe it is cut from its stalks. This is called reaping.

- **After reaping** the grain must be separated from the stalks and chaff (waste). This is called threshing.

- **After threshing** the grain must be cleaned and separated from the husks. This is called winnowing.

- **In some places** grain is still reaped in the ancient way with a long curved blade called a sickle.

- **In most developed countries** wheat and other cereals are usually harvested with a combine harvester.

- **A combine harvester** is a machine that reaps the grain, threshes it, cleans it and pours it into bags or reservoirs.

- **The first horse-drawn** combine was used in Michigan in 1836, but modern self-propelled harvesters only came into use in the 1940s.

- **If the grain is damp** it must be dried immediately after harvesting so it does not rot. This is always true of rice.

▲ Combine harvesters driven by a single man have replaced the huge teams of people with sickles of ancient times.

- **If the grain is too damp** to harvest, a machine called a windrower may cut the stalks and lay them in rows to dry in the wind for later threshing and cleaning.

- **A successful harvest** is traditionally celebrated with a harvest festival. The cailleac or last sheaf of corn is said to be the spirit of the field. It is made into a harvest doll, drenched with water and saved for the spring planting.

Desert plants

▲ Surprisingly, many plants can survive the dryness of deserts, including cactuses and sagebushes.

- **Some plants** find water in the dry desert with very long roots. The Mesquite has roots that can go down as much as 50 m deep.

- **Most desert plants** have tough waxy leaves to cut down on water loss. They also have very few leaves; cactuses have none at all.

- **Pebble plants** avoid the desert heat by growing partly underground.

- **Window plants** grow almost entirely underground. A long cigar shape pokes into the ground, with just a small green window on the surface to catch sunlight.

- **Some mosses and lichens** get water by soaking up dew.

- **Resurrection trees** get their name because their leaves look shrivelled brown and dead most of the time – then suddenly turn green when it rains.

- **The rose of Jericho** is a resurrection plant that forms a dry ball that lasts for years and opens only when damp.

- **Daisies** are found in most deserts.

- **Cactuses and ice plants** can store water for many months in special water storage organs.

★ STAR FACT ★
The quiver tree drops its branches to save water in times of drought.

Fungi

- **Fungi** are a huge group of 50,000 species. They include mushrooms, toadstools, mould, mildew and yeast.

- **Fungi** are not plants, because they have no chlorophyll to make their food. So scientists put them in a group or kingdom of their own.

- **Because fungi** cannot make their own food, they must live off other plants and animals – sometimes as partners, sometimes as parasites.

- **Parasitic fungi** feed off living organisms; fungi that live off dead plants and animals are called saprophytic.

- **Fungi** feed by releasing chemicals called enzymes to break down chemicals in their host. The fungi then use the chemicals as food.

▶ These are some of the tens of thousands of different fungi, which are found growing everywhere from rotting tree stumps to inside your body.

- **Cheeses** like Camembert, Rocquefort, Stilton and Danish Blue get their distinctive flavours from chemicals made by moulds added to them to help them ripen. The blue streaks in some cheeses are actually moulds.

- **Fungi are made** of countless cotton-like threads called hyphae which absorb the chemicals they feed on. Hyphae are usually spread out in a tangled mass. But they can bundle together to form fruiting bodies like mushrooms.

- **Some fungi** grow by spreading their hyphae in a mat or mycelium; others scatter their spores. Those that grow from spores go through the same two stages as mosses.

- **Truffles** are fungi that grow near oak and hazel roots. They are prized for their flavour and sniffed out by dogs or pigs. The best come from Perigord in France.

The field mushroom, grown wild or cultivated, is the mushroom most widely eaten

Honey mushrooms belong to the Armillaria genus of fungi, which includes the world's largest and oldest living organisms

Fungi can grow in all kinds of shapes, earning them names like this orange peel fungi

The destroying angel is the most poisonous of all fungi, and usually kills anyone who eats one

The water-measure earthstar grows in soil or on rotting wood in grassy areas or woods

Fly agaric is a toadstool – that is, a poisonous mushroom. It is easy to recognize from its spotted red cap

The chanterelle is a sweet-smelling, edible amber-coloured mushroom. But it looks very like the poisonous jack o'lantern

Puffballs have big round fruiting bodies that dry out and puff out their spores in all directions when burst

Heathlands

▲ *Heather and other heathland plants are usually pollinated by bees and birds such as sunbirds.*

- **Heathland** goes under many different names, including scrubland, shrubland and chaparral.

- **Heathlands** occur where the soil is too dry or too poor for trees to grow – typically in Mediterranean regions or areas of sandy soil.

- **Many heathlands** are not natural, but places where human activity has so changed the environment that trees can no longer grow.

- **The most common** heathland shrub is heather. Underneath grasses, sedges and flowers like daisies and orchids grow.

- **Many heathland shrubs** like gorse are thorny to stop animals eating them.

- **The maquis** are the heathlands of the Mediterranean, dominated by tough evergreen shrubs and small trees.

- **Many maquis** plants are aromatic (have a strong scent) – such as mints, laurels and myrtles.

- **Spring blossoms** in the mallee heaths of Australia are so spectacular that they are a tourist attraction.

- **Mallee** is a kind of eucalyptus tree typical of the area.

- **Chaparral** is heathland in California. The climate is Mediterranean, with mild winters and warm summers. The main plants are sages and small evergreen oaks.

Timber

- **Timber** is useful wood. Lumber is a North American term for timber once it is sawn or split.

- **Lumberjacks** are people who cut down trees using power saws or chainsaws.

- **Round timbers** are basically tree trunks that have been stripped of their bark and branches and cut into logs.

- **Round timbers** are used for fencing and telegraph poles or driven into the ground as 'piles' to support buildings and quays.

- **Lumber** is boards and planks sawn from logs at sawmills. At least half of lumber is used for building.

▲ *Tree surgeons stripping branches from a felled tree with chainsaws.*

- **Before lumber** can be used, it must usually be seasoned (dried) or it will shrink or twist. Sometimes it is dried in the open air, but more often it is warmed in a kiln or treated with chemicals.

- **Sometimes** planks are cut into thin slices called veneers.

- **Plywood** is three or more veneers glued together to make cheap, strong wood. Chipboard is wood chippings and sawdust mixed with glue and pressed into sheets.

- **Softwod lumbers** come from trees such as pines, larches, firs, hemlocks, redwoods and cedars.

- **MDF** or medium density fibreboard is made from glued wood fibres.

Symbiosis

- **Living things** that feed off other living things are called parasites.

- **Living things** that depend on each other to live are called symbiotic.

- **Many tropical rainforest trees** have a symbiotic relationship with fungi on their roots. The fungi get

▼ *Leaf-cutter ants cut up leaves and line their nests – not for themselves, but for the fungi that grow on the leaves. The ants eat the fungi.*

energy from the trees and in return give the trees phosphorus and other nutrients.

- **A phyte is a plant** that grows on another plant.

- **Epiphytes** are plants that grow high up on other plants, especially in tropical rainforests (see epiphytes).

- **Saprophytes** are plants and fungi that depend on decomposing material, not sunlight, for sustenance.

- **Most orchids** are saprophytic as seedlings.

- **Corsiaceae orchids** of New Guinea, Australia and Chile are saprophytic all their lives.

- **Various ants**, such as leaf-cutter and harvester ants in tropical forests, line their nests with leaves which they cut up. The leaves provide food for fungi which, in turn, provide food for the ants.

Tree flowers

- **All trees have flowers**, but the flowers of conifers are usually tiny compared with those of broad-leaved trees.

- **Flowers** are a tree's reproductive organs.

- **Some flowers are male.** Some are female.

- **Sometimes the male** and female flowers are on separate trees. Sometimes, as in willows and some conifers, they are on the same tree.

- **'Perfect' flowers** like those of cherry and maple trees have both male and female parts.

- **Pollen** is carried from male flowers by insects or the wind to fertilize female flowers.

- **A blossom** can be any flower, but often refers especially to the beautiful flowers of fruit trees such as cherries and apples in spring.

- **Many blossoms** are pink and get their colour from what are called anthocyanin pigments – the same chemical colours that turn leaves red in autumn.

- **Washington DC** is famous for its Cherry Blossom Festival each spring.

- **Omiya** in Japan is famous for its park full of cherry trees which blossom in spring.

▼ *Apple blossoms are usually pink. They bloom quite late in spring, after both peach and cherry blossoms.*

Parts of a plant

All plants that grow from seeds have flowers, although not all are as bright and colourful as these

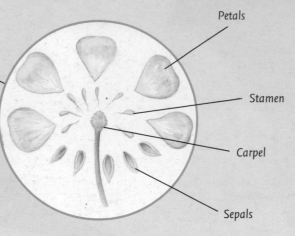

Petals

Stamen

Carpel

Sepals

Flowers usually open only for a short time. Before they open, they are hidden in tight green buds

The leaves are the plant's powerhouses, using sunlight to make sugar, the plant's fuel

◄ Plants come in many shapes and sizes from tiny wildflowers to giant trees 100 m tall. But they all tend to have the same basic features – roots, stem, leaves and flowers.

The stem supports the leaves and flowers and channels water and minerals up from the roots

The roots grow down into soil or water. They hold the plant in place, and allow it to draw up water and minerals

- **The first plants** to appear on land were simple plants such as liverworts, ferns and horsetails. They grow from tiny cells called spores.

- **Today, most plants** grow not from spores but from seeds. Unlike primitive plants, seed-making plants have stems, leaves and often roots and flowers.

- **The stem of a plant** supports the leaves and flowers. It also carries water, minerals and food up and down between the plant's leaves and roots.

- **A terminal bud** forms the tip of each stem. The plant grows taller here.

- **Lateral buds** grow further back down the stem at places called nodes.

- **Some lateral buds** develop into new branches. Others develop into leaves or flowers.

- **The leaves** are the plant's green surfaces for catching sunlight. They use the sun's energy for joining water with carbon dioxide from the air to make the sugar the plant needs to grow (see photosynthesis).

- **The roots** are the parts of the plant that grow down into soil or water. They anchor the plant in the ground and soak up all the water and minerals it needs to grow.

- **The flowers** are the plant's reproductive organs. In gymnosperms – conifers, cycads and gingkos – the flowers are often small and hidden. In angiosperms (flowering plants) they are usually much more obvious.

Tropical trees

◀ *Mangrove trees are famous for their dangling pods that can drop like a sword on passersby.*

- **Nearly all tropical trees** are broad-leaved trees.

- **Most tropical trees** are evergreen. Only where there is a marked dry season in 'monsoon' regions do some trees loose their leaves to save water.

- **Most tropical trees** are slow-growing hardwoods such as teak and mahogany. Once cut down, they take many years to replace.

★ STAR FACT ★
Balsa wood from Central America is the lightest and softest wood of all.

- **Mahogany** is a tall evergreen tree with beautiful hard wood that turns red when it matures after a century or so.

- **Most mahogany** wood comes from trees such as the African *Khaya* or the *Shorea* from the Philippines.

- **The best mahogany** is from the tropical American *Swietenia macrophylla*.

- **Balsa** is so light and such a good insulator that it is used to make passenger compartments in aircraft.

- **Teak** is a deciduous tree from India. It is one of the toughest of all woods and has been used to construct ships and buildings for more than 2000 years.

- **Chicle** is a gum drained from the Central American sapota tree in the rainy season. It is the main ingredient in chewing-gum. The best comes from Guatemala.

Dandelions and daisies

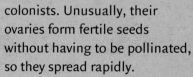

- **Dandelions and daisies** are both members of a vast family called *Asteraceae*.

- **All *Asteraceae*** have flower heads with many small flowers called florets surrounded by leaf-like structures called bracts.

- **There are over 20,000** different *Asteraceae*.

- **Garden *Asteraceae*** include asters, dahlias and chrysanthemums.

- **Wild *Asteraceae*** include burdock, butterbur and ragweed, thistles and sagebrush.

▶ *Daisies look like a single bloom, but they actually consist of many small flowers. Those around the edge each have a single petal.*

- **Lettuces, artichokes** and sunflowers are all *Asteraceae*.

- **The thistle** is the national emblem of Scotland.

- **Dandelions** are bright yellow flowers that came originally from Europe, but were taken to America by colonists. Unusually, their ovaries form fertile seeds without having to be pollinated, so they spread rapidly.

- **The name dandelion** comes from the French *dent de lion*, meaning lion's tooth – because its leaves have edges that look like sharp teeth.

- **The daisy** gets its name from the Old English words 'day's eye' – because like an eye its blooms open in the day and close at night.

Berries

- **Berries** are fleshy fruit that contain lots of seeds. The bright colours attract birds, which eat the flesh. The seeds pass out in the birds' droppings and so spread.

- **Bananas**, tomatoes and cranberries are all berries.

- **Strawberries**, raspberries and blackberries are not true berries. They are called 'aggregate' fruits because each is made from groups of tiny fruit with one seed.

- **Gean, damson and blackthorn berries** contain a single seed. Holly berries and elderberries contain many.

- **Cloudberries** are aggregate fruits like raspberries. The tiny amber berries grow close to the ground in the far north, and are collected by Inuits and Sami people in autumn to freeze for winter food.

◀ *Most berries are shiny bright red to attract birds.*

- **Cloudberries** are also known as salmonberries, bakeberries, malka and baked appleberries.

- **Cranberries** grow wild on small trailing plants in marshes, but are now cultivated extensively in the USA in places such as Massachusetts.

- **Wild huckleberries** are the American version of the European bilberry. But the evergreen huckleberry sold in florists is actually a blueberry.

- **The strawberry tree's** Latin name is *unedo*, which means 'I eat one'. The red berries are not as tasty as they look.

- **A Greek myth** tells how the wine-red mulberry was once white but was stained red by the blood of the tragic lovers Pyramus and Thisbe, whose story is retold in Shakespeare's *Midsummer Night's Dream*.

Ash trees

- **Ash trees** are 70 species of deciduous trees that grow through much of northern Eurasia and North America.

- **Ash trees** are among the most beautiful of all trees and are prized for their wood. It was once used to make oars and handles for axes, tennis rackets and skis.

- **The tallest of all flowering plants** is the Australian mountain ash, which grows over 100 m tall.

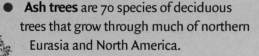

◀ *The leaves of the ash grow opposite each other in groups of five to nine and have tooth edges. The clusters of flowers are small and often showy.*

- **Ash trees** are part of the olive family.

- **The Vikings** worshipped the ash as a sacred tree. Yggdrasil, the Tree of the World, was a giant ash whose roots reached into hell but whose crown reached heaven.

- **In Viking myth** Odin, the greatest of the gods, created the first man out of a piece of ash wood.

- **The manna ash** got its name because it was once thought that its sugary gum was manna. Manna was the miraculous food that fell from heaven to feed the Biblical Children of Israel in the desert as they fled from Egypt.

- **The mountain ash** is also known as the rowan or quickbeam. In America it is known as dogberry. It is not related to other ash trees.

- **Rowan trees** were once linked to witchcraft. The name may come from the Viking word *runa*, meaning charm. Rowan trees were planted in churchyards, and the berries were hung over doors on May Day, to ward off evil.

- **Rowans** grow higher up mountains than any other tree.

Dicotyledons

▲▶ Dicots, like the Japanese maple above, all begin life as a pair of leaves growing from a seed, like those on the right.

- **Dicotyledons** are one of two basic classes of flowering plant. The other is monocotyledons.

- **Dicotyledons** are also known as dicots or Magnoliopsida.

- **Dicots** are plants that sprout two leaves from their seeds.

- **There are about 175,000** dicots – over three-quarters of all flowering plants.

- **Dicots** include most garden plants, shrubs and trees as well as flowers such as magnolias, roses, geraniums and hollyhocks.

- **Dicots** grow slowly and at least 50 percent have woody stems.

- **The flowers** of dicots have sets of four or five petals.

- **Most dicots** have branching stems and a single main root called a taproot.

- **The leaves of dicots** usually have a network of veins rather than parallel veins.

- **Dicots** usually have a layer of ever-growing cells near the outside of the stem called the cambium.

Orchids

- **Orchids** are a group of over 20,000 species of flower, growing on every continent but Antarctica.

- **In the moist tropics** many grow on the trunks and branches of trees and so are called epiphytes.

- **A few**, such as the Bird's nest orchid, are saprophytes, living off rotting plants in places where there is no light.

- **Some species** are found throughout the tropics, such as *Ionopsis utricularioides*. Others grow on just a single mountain in the world.

- **Orchids** have a big central petal called the lip or labellum. It is often shaped like a cup, trumpet or bag.

- **The fly orchid** of Ecuador has a lip shaped like a female tachinid fly to attract male flies.

- **The flavour vanilla** comes from the vanilla orchid.

- **Ancient Greek** couples expecting a baby often ate the roots of the early purple orchid. They believed that if the man ate the flower's large root the baby would be a boy. If the woman ate the small root, the baby would be a girl.

- **In Shakespeare's** *Hamlet*, the drowned Ophelia is covered in flowers, including the early purple orchid, famous as a love potion. Hamlet's mother says that 'cold maids' call the flowers 'dead men's fingers'.

▶The early purple orchid was said to have grown beneath Christ's cross and the red spots on its leaves were said to be left by falling drops of Christ's blood.

Cycads and gingkos

- **Cycadophytes and gingkophytes** were the first seed plants to appear on land. The cycads and gingkos of today are their direct descendants.

- **Like conifers**, cycads and gingkos are gymnosperms. This means their seeds do not develop inside a fruit like those of flowering plants or angiosperms.

- **Cycads** are mostly short, stubby, palm-like trees. Some are many thousands of years old.

- **Cycads have** fern-like leaves growing in a circle round the end of the stem. New leaves sprout each year and last for several years.

- **The gingko** is a tall tree that comes from China.

- **The gingko** is the only living gingkophyte.

- **The gingko** is the world's oldest living seed-plant.

- **Fossil leaves** identical to today's gingko have been found all over the world in rocks formed in the Jurassic Period, 208–144 million years ago.

▲ The gingko is a remarkable living fossil – the only living representative of the world's most ancient seed plants.

- **Scientifically,** the gingko is called *Gingko Biloba*. It is also called the maidenhair tree.

- **Today's** gingkos may be descended from trees first cultivated in Chinese temple gardens 3000 years ago.

River plants

▲ Water crowfoots are buttercups that grow in water. They may have both round floating leaves like these and feathery submerged leaves.

- **Some aquatic (water) plants** are rooted in the mud and have their leaves above the surface like water lilies.

- **Some water plants** grow underwater but for their flowers, like water milfoils and some plantains. They may have bladders or air pockets to help keep the stem upright.

- **Tiny plants** called algae grow in red, green or brown films on rivers, lakes and swamps.

- **Water hyacinths** are purple American water flowers. They grow quickly and can clog up slow streams.

- **Giant water lilies** have huge leaves with the edges upturned like a shallow pan to keep them afloat.

- **The leaves** of the royal or Amazon lily can be 2 m across.

- **Papyrus** is a tall, grass-like water plant that grows in the Nile river. Stems were rolled flat by the ancient Egyptians to write on. The word 'paper' comes from papyrus.

- **Many grass-like** plants grow in water, including reeds, mace, flag and rushes such as bulrushes and cattails.

- **Mangroves, bald cypresses**, cotton gum and other 'hydrophytic' trees are adapted to living in water.

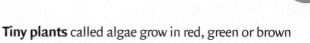

> ★ STAR FACT ★
> Mexico's largest lake, Lake Chapala, is sometimes choked with water hyacinths.

Development of a flower

- **Flowers have both** male parts, called stamens, and female parts, called carpels. Seeds for new plants are made when pollen from the stamens meets the flower's eggs inside the carpels.

- **The carpel** contains the ovaries, where the flower's eggs are made. It is typically the short thick stalk in the middle of the flower.

  - **A flower** may have just one carpel or several joined together. Together, they are called the pistil.

    - **The stamens** make pollen. They are typically spindly stalks surrounding the carpels.

    - **Pollen is made** in the anthers on top of the stamens.

    - **Pollen** is trapped on the top of the ovary by sticky stigma.

1. The fully formed flower is packed away inside a bud. Green flaps or sepals wrap tightly round it

2. Once the weather is warm enough, the bud begins to open. The sepals curl back to reveal the colourful petals

3. The sepals open wider and the petals grow outwards and backwards to create the flower's beautiful corolla

▶ *At the right time of year, buds begin to open to reveal flowers' blooms so that the reproductive process can begin. Some flowers last just a day or so. Others stay blooming for months on end before the eggs are fertilized, and grow into seeds.*

4. The flower opens fully to reveal its bright array of pollen sacs

▶ *Most flowers rely on bees and butterflies to fertilize them by transferring pollen from the stamens to the carpels. So, like this orchid, flowers have developed wonderful colours and scents to attract the insects to them.*

- **Pollen** is carried down to the ovary from the stigma via a structure called the style. In the ovary it meets the eggs and fertilizes them to create seeds.

- **Before the flower opens,** the bud is enclosed in a tight green ball called the calyx. This is made up from tiny green flaps called sepals.

- **The colourful part of the flower** is made from groups of petals. The petals make up what is called the corolla. Together the calyx and the corolla make up the whole flower head, which is called the perianth. If petals and sepals are the same colour, they are said to be tepals.

> ★ STAR FACT ★
> A 'perfect' flower is one which has both stamens and carpels; many have one missing.

Deciduous trees

◀ In autumn, the leaves of deciduous trees turn glorious browns, reds and golds and then drop off. New leaves grow in the spring.

● **Deciduous trees** are trees that lose their leaves once a year.

● **In cool places**, deciduous trees lose their leaves in autumn to cut their need for water in winter when water may be frozen.

● **In the tropics** deciduous trees lose their leaves at the start of the dry season.

● **Leaves fall** because a layer of cork grows across the leaf stalk, gradually cutting off its water supply.

● **Eventually the leaf** is only hanging on by its veins, and is easily blown off by the wind.

● **Leaves go brown** and other colours in autumn because their green chlorophyll breaks down, letting other pigments shine through instead.

● **Among the most spectacular** autumn colours are those of the sweet gum, brought to Europe from Mexico c.1570.

● **The main deciduous trees** in cool climates are oaks, beeches, birches, chestnuts, aspens, elms, maples and lindens.

● **Most deciduous trees** are broad-leaved, but five conifer groups including larches are deciduous.

● **Some tropical evergreen trees** are deciduous in regions where there is a marked dry season.

Tree leaves

● **Trees** can be divided into two groups according to their leaves: broad-leaved trees and conifers with needle-like leaves.

● **The leaves** of broad-leaved trees are all wide and flat to catch the sun, but they vary widely in shape.

● **You can identify** trees by their leaves. Features to look for are not only the overall shape, but also the number of leaflets on the same stalk, whether leaflets are paired or offset and if there are teeth round the edges of the leaves.

● **Trees such as birches** and poplars have small triangular or 'deltoid' leaves; aspens and alders have round leaves.

● **Limes** and Indian bean trees have heart-shaped or 'cordate' leaves.

Lobed leaves of the English oak

Hand-shaped leaf of a horse chestnut

Long, narrow willow leaves

● **Maples** and sycamores have leaves shaped a bit like hands, which is why they are called 'palmate'.

● **Ash and walnut trees** have lots of leaflets on the same stalk, giving them a feathery or 'pinnate' look.

● **Oaks and whitebeams** have leaves indented with lobes round the edge.

● **Many shrubs,** like magnolias and buddleias, and trees like willows, cherries, sweet chestnuts and cork oaks, have long narrow leaves.

● **Elms, beeches,** pears, alders and many others have oval leaves.

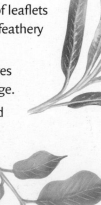

Pinnate or feather-shaped walnut leaves

Root vegetables

▲▶ *Potatoes and carrots are important root vegetables. Carrot is a source of vitamin A, potatoes are sources of many vitamins, such as C.*

- **Vegetables** are basically any part of a plant eaten cooked or raw, except for the fruit.
- **Root vegetables** are parts of a plant that grow underground in the soil.

- **Turnips, rutabaga**, beets, carrots, parsnips and sweet potatoes are the actual roots of the plant.
- **Potatoes and cassava** are tubers or storage stems.
- **Potatoes** were grown in South America at least 1800 years ago. They were brought to Europe by the Spanish in the 16th century.
- **Poor Irish** farmers came to depend on the potato, and when blight ruined the crop in the 1840s, many starved.
- **Yams are tropical roots** similar to sweet potatoes. They are an important food in West Africa. A single yam can weigh 45 kg or more.
- **Mangel-wurzels** are beet plants grown mainly to feed to farm animals.
- **Tapioca** is a starchy food made from cassava that once made popular puddings.
- **Carrots came** originally from Afghanistan, but were spread around the Mediterranean 4000 years ago. They reached China by the 13th century AD.

Poisonous fungi

- **Many fungi** produce poisons. Scientists call poisons 'toxins' and poisons made by fungi 'mycotoxins'.
- **Some poisonous fungi** are very small microfungi which often form moulds or mildew. Many are either 'sac' fungi (*Ascomycetes*) or 'imperfect' fungi (*Deuteromycetes*).
- **Ergot** is a disease of cereals, especially rye, caused by the sac fungus *Claviceps purpurea*. If humans eat ergot-infected rye, they may suffer an illness called St Anthony's Fire. Ergot is also the source of the drug LSD.
- **Aspergillus** is an imperfect fungus that may cause liver damage or even cancer in humans.
- **False morel** is a poisonous sac fungus as big as a mushroom. True morels are harmless.
- **About 75 kinds** of mushroom are toxic to humans and

so called toadstools. Most belong to the Amanita family, including destroying angels, death caps and fly agarics.

- **Death caps** contain deadly phalline toxins that kill most people who eat the fungus.
- **Fly agaric** was once used as fly poison.
- **Fly agaric** and the *Psilocybe mexicana* mushroom were eaten by Latin American Indians because they gave hallucinations.

▶ *Fly agaric contains the poison muscarine. It rarely kills but makes you sick and agitated.*

★ STAR FACT ★
Athlete's foot is a nasty foot condition caused by a fungus.

Broad-leaved woodlands

▲ *Avenues of broad-leaved trees form shady paths in summer but are light in winter when the trees are bare.*

- **Forests** of broad-leaved, deciduous trees grow in temperate regions where there are warm, wet summers and cold winters – in places like North America, western Europe and eastern Asia.

- **Broad-leaved deciduous** woods grow where temperatures average above 10°C for over six months a year, and the average annual rainfall is over 400 mm.

▼ *Plenty of light can filter down through deciduous trees – especially in winter when the leaves are gone – so all kinds of bushes and flowers grow in the woods, often blooming in spring while the leaves are still thin.*

- **If there are** 100 to 200 days a year warm enough for growth, the main trees in broad-leaved deciduous forests are oaks, elms, birches, maples, beeches, aspens, chestnuts and lindens (basswood).

- **In the tropics** where there is plenty of rainfall, broad-leaved evergreens form tropical rainforests.

- **In moist western Europe,** beech trees dominate woods on well-drained, shallow soils, especially chalkland; oak trees prefer deep clay soils. Alders grow in waterlogged places.

- **In drier eastern Europe,** beeches are replaced by durmast oak and hornbeam and in Russia by lindens.

- **In American woods,** beech and linden are rarer than in Europe, but oaks, hickories and maples are more common.

- **In the Appalachians** buckeye and tulip trees dominate.

- **There is a wide range** of shrubs under the trees including dogwood, holly, magnolia, as well as woodland flowers.

> ★ STAR FACT ★
> Very few woods in Europe are entirely natural; most are 'secondary' woods, growing on land once cleared for farms.

Cut flowers

◀ The Netherlands is still famous for its flower markets.

● **Cut flowers** are flowers sold by the bunch in florists.

● **The cut flower** trade began in the Netherlands with tulips in the 1600s.

● **In 1995** 60 percent of the world's cut flowers were grown in the Netherlands.

● **Latin American countries** like Columbia, Ecuador, Guatemala and Costa Rica are now major flower-growers. So too are African countries like Kenya, Zimbabwe, South Africa, Zambia and Tanzania.

● **In China** the growing popularity of St Valentine's day has meant huge areas of China are now planted with flowers.

● **After cutting**, flowers are chilled and sent by air to arrive in places like Europe and North America fresh.

● **Most of the world's** cut flowers are sold through the huge flower market in Rotterdam in the Netherlands.

● **By encouraging** certain flowers, flower-growers have made cut flowers last longer in the vase – but they have lost the rich scents they once had. Scientists are now trying to reintroduce scent genes to flowers.

● **A corsage** is a small bouquet women began to wear on their waists in the 18th century.

● **A nosegay** was a small bouquet Victorian ladies carried in their hands. If a man gave a lady a red tulip it meant he loved her. If she gave him back a sprig of dogwood it meant she didn't care. Various pink flowers meant 'no'.

Wheat

● **Wheat grows** over more farmland than any other crop and is the basic food for 35 percent of the population.

● **Wheat was** one of the first crops ever grown, planted by the first farmers some 11,000 years ago.

● **Today** there are over 30 varieties. Among the oldest are emmer and einkorn.

● **Spring wheat** is planted in spring and then harvested in early autumn.

● **Winter wheat** is planted in autumn and harvested the following summer.

● **Wheat** is a kind of grass, along with other cereals.

● **Young wheat plants** are short and green and look like ordinary grass, but as they ripen they turn golden and grow between 0.6 and 1.5 m tall.

● **Branching from the main stem** are stalks called tillers. Wrapped round them is the base or sheath of the leaves. The flat top of the leaf is called the blade.

● **The head of the corn** where the seeds or grain grow is called the ear or spike. We eat the seed's kernels (core), ground into flour to make bread, pasta and other things.

▼ An ear of wheat with the seeds which are stripped of their shells or husks before being ground to make flour.

Annuals and biennials

▲ *Foxgloves are typical biennials, flowering in their second summer, then dying back.*

- **Annuals** are plants that grow from seed, flower, disperse their seeds and die in a single season.

- **Some annuals' seeds** lie dormant in the ground before conditions are right for germination.

- **With an annual**, forming flowers, fruits and seeds exhausts the plant's food reserves so the green parts die.

- **Many crops** are annuals, including peas and beans, squashes, and cereals such as maize and wheat.

- **Annual flowers** include petunias, lobelias, buttercups and delphiniums.

- **Biennials** live for two years.

- **In the first year** the young plant grows a ring of leaves and builds up an underground food store such as a bulb or taproot like beetroots and carrots. The food store sustains the plant through the winter.

- **In the second year** the plant sends up a stem in spring. It flowers in the summer.

- **Many vegetables** are biennials, including beetroot, carrots and turnips.

- **Biennial flowers** include wallflowers, carnations, sweet williams and evening primroses.

Bamboo

- **Bamboos** are giant, fast-growing grasses with woody stems.

- **Most bamboos** grow in east and southeast Asia and on islands in the Indian and Pacific oceans.

- **Bamboo stems** are called culms. They often form dense thickets that exclude every other plant.

- **Bamboo culms** can reach up to 40 m and grow very fast. Some bamboos grow 1 m every three days.

- **Most bamboos** only flower every 12 years or so. Some flower only 30–60 years. *Phyllostachys bambusoides* flowers only after 120 years.

- **Pandas** depend on the *Phyllostachys* bamboo, and after it flowers they lose their source of food.

▲ *Bamboo looks like trees with its tall woody stems and big leaves, but it is actually grass.*

- **The flowering** of the muli bamboo around the Bay of Bengal every 30–35 years brings disaster as rats multiply to take advantage of the fruit.

- **The Chinese** have used the hollow stems of bamboo to make flutes since before the Stone Age. The Australian aboriginals use them to make droning pipes called didgeridoos.

- **Bamboo** is an incredibly light, strong material, and between 1904 and 1957 athletes used it for pole-vaulting. American Cornelius Warmerdam vaulted 4.77 m with a bamboo pole.

- **Bamboo** has long been used to make paper. The Bamboo Annals, written on bamboo, are the oldest written Chinese records, dating from the 8th century BC.

Citrus fruit

- **Citrus fruits** are a group of juicy soft fruits covered with a very thick, waxy, evenly coloured skin in yellow, orange or green.

- **Citrus** fruits include lemons, limes, oranges, tangerines, grapefruits and shaddocks.

▼ *Orange trees are planted in groves. The fruit are green when they first appear, but turn orange as they ripen.*

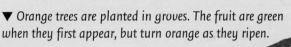

★ STAR FACT ★
Citrus fruits are richer in Vitamin C than any other fruit or vegetable.

- **Inside the skin,** the flesh of a citrus fruit is divided into clear segments, each usually containing one or several seeds or pips.

- **Citrus fruits** grow in warm Mediterranean climates, and they are very vulnerable to frost.

- **Some citrus** fruit-growers warm the trees with special burners in winter to avoid frost-damage.

- **The sharp tang** of citrus fruits comes from citric acid.

- **Lemons** were spread through Europe by the crusaders who found them growing in Palestine.

- **Columbus** took limes to the Americas in 1493.

- **Scottish physician** James Lind (1716-1794) helped eradicate the disease scurvy from the British navy by recommending that sailors eat oranges and lemons.

Parasites

- **Parasitic plants** are plants that get their food not by using sunlight but from other plants, at the others' expense.

- **In the gloom of** tropical rainforests, where sunlight cannot penetrate, there are many parasitic plants growing on the trees.

- **Lianas** save themselves energy growing a trunk by climbing up other trees, clinging on with little hooks.

- **Rafflesia,** the world's biggest flower, is a parasite that feeds on the roots of lianas.

- **Figs** begin growing from seeds left high on branches by birds or fruit bats.

- **Fig roots** grow down to the ground around the tree, strangling it by taking its water supply. The tree then dies away, leaving the fig roots as a hollow 'trunk'.

- **Mistletoes** are semi-parasitic plants that wind round trees. They draw some of their food from the tree and some from sunlight with their own leaves.

- **Viscum album** mistletoe was held sacred by Druids 2000 years ago.

- **The druid** belief in the magic power of mistletoe survives in the tradition of kissing under the mistletoe at Christmas.

- **Broomrapes** grow on sugarcane roots; witchweeds grow on maize and rice roots.

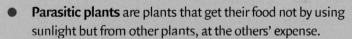

◄ *Mistletoe, with its distinctive white berries, grows on apple and poplar trees in Eurasia and oaks in America.*

Epiphytes

- **Epiphytes** are plants that grow high above the ground in tropical rainforests, on tree branches.

- **Epiphytes** are often known as air plants because they seem to live on air – attached neither to the ground nor to any obvious source of nutrients.

- **Epiphytes** get their water and minerals from rain water, and from debris on the branch.

- **Various** orchids, ferns and bromeliads are epiphytes in tropical forests.

- **There are also epiphytes** in cooler places, including lichens, mosses, liverworts and algae.

- **Bromeliads** belong to a big family of plants called the pineapple family. At least half of them are epiphytes.

- **The pineapple fruit** is the best-known bromeliad.

- **All but one bromeliad** come from America, but they live in a huge range of habitats, living anywhere from on cacti in deserts to moist forests high up mountains.

▲ Trees in tropical rainforests are often covered in epiphytes festooned on every bough and branch.

- **The smallest bromeliads** are moss-like *Tillandsia bryoides*, just a few centimetres long.

- **The biggest bromeliad** is *Puya raimondii*, with a stem up to 4 m long and a flower over 4 m tall.

Seeds and nuts

- **Seeds are the tiny** hard capsules from which most new plants grow.

- **Seeds** develop from the plant's egg once it is fertilized by pollen.

- **Each seed** contains the new plant in embryo form plus a store of food to feed it until it grows leaves.

- ●**The seed** is wrapped in a hard shell or testa.

◄ Neither Brazil nuts nor coconuts are true nuts. Coconuts (right) are the stones of drupes. Brazil nuts (left) are just large seeds.

- **Some fruit** contain many seeds; nuts are fruit with a single seed in which the outside has gone hard.

- **Acorns and hazelnuts** are true nuts.

- **Cola drinks** get their name from the African kola nut, but there are no nuts in them. The flavour is artificial.

- **Some nuts**, such as almonds and walnuts, are not true nuts but the hard stones of drupes (fruit like plums).

- **Brazil nuts** and shelled peanuts are not true nuts but just large seeds.

- **Nuts are** a concentrated, nutritious food – about 50 percent fat and 10–20 percent protein. Peanuts contain more energy than sugar and more protein, minerals and vitamins than liver.

▶ Almonds come from trees native to SW Asia but are now grown all over the world.

Photosynthesis

- **Plants use** sunlight to chemically join carbon dioxide gas from the air with water to make sugary food. The process is called photosynthesis.

- **Photosynthesis** occurs in leaves in two special kinds of cell: palisade and spongy cells.

- **Inside the palisade** and spongy cells are tiny packages called chloroplasts. A chloroplast is like a little bag with a double skin or membrane. Each is filled with a jelly-like substance called the stroma in which float various structures, such as lamellae. The jelly contains a chemical called chlorophyll that makes leaves green.

- **The leaf** draws in air containing the gas carbon dioxide through pores called stomata. It also draws water up from the ground through the stem and veins.

- **When the sun** is shining, the chlorophyll soaks up its energy and uses it to split water into hydrogen and oxygen. The hydrogen released from the water combines with the carbon dioxide to make sugar; the oxygen goes out through the stomata.

- **Sugar is transported** around the plant to where it is needed. Some sugar is burned up at once, leaving carbon dioxide and water. This is called respiration.

> ★ STAR FACT ★
> The oxygen in the air on which we depend for life was all made by plants during photosynthesis.

- **Some sugar is combined** into large molecules called starches, which are easy for the plant to store. The plant breaks these starches down into sugars again whenever they are needed as fuel.

- **Starch** from plants is the main nutrient we get when we eat food such as bread, rice and potatoes. When we eat fruits, cakes or anything else sweet, the sweetness comes from sugar made by photosynthesis.

- **Together** all the world's plants produce about 150 billion tonnes of sugar each year by photosynthesis.

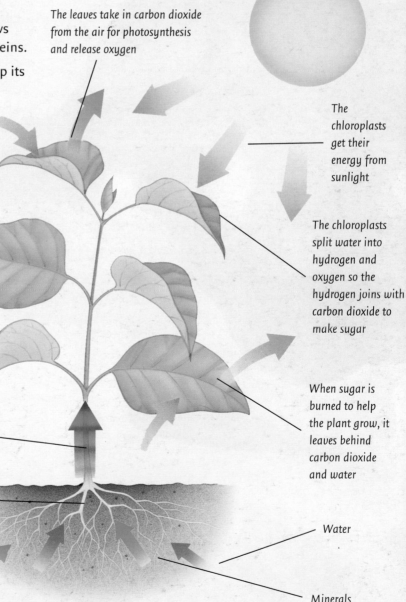

The leaves take in carbon dioxide from the air for photosynthesis and release oxygen

The chloroplasts get their energy from sunlight

The chloroplasts split water into hydrogen and oxygen so the hydrogen joins with carbon dioxide to make sugar

When sugar is burned to help the plant grow, it leaves behind carbon dioxide and water

The minerals are carried up through the plant dissolved in the water

The plant takes up water and minerals from the soil through the roots

Water

Minerals

▶ Every green plant is a remarkable chemical factory, taking in energy from the sun and using it to split water into hydrogen and oxygen. It then combines the hydrogen with carbon dioxide from the air to make sugar, the fuel the plant needs to grow.

Tree facts

▲ *General Sherman in California is the biggest living tree. It is a giant sequoia over 83 m tall and with a trunk 11 m across.*

- **The biggest tree** ever known was the Lindsey Creek Tree, a massive redwood that blew over in 1905. It weighed over 3300 tonnes.

- **The tallest living tree** is the 112 m high Mendocino redwood tree in Montgomery State Reserve, California.

- **The tallest tree** ever known was a Eucalyptus on Watts River, Victoria, Australia, measured at over 150 m in 1872.

- **The great banyan** tree in the Indian Botanical Garden, Calcutta has a canopy covering 1.2 hectares.

- **Banyan trees** grow trunk-like roots from their branches.

- **A European chestnut** known as the Tree of the Hundred Horses on Mt Etna in Sicily had a girth (the distance round the trunk) of 57.9 m in the 1790s.

- **A Moctezuma baldcypress** near Oaxaca in Mexico has a trunk over 12 m across.

- **The world's oldest plant** is the King's Holly in southwestern Tasmania, thought to be 43,000 years old.

- **The ombu tree** of Argentina is the world's toughest tree, able to survive axes, fire, storms and insect attacks.

> ★ **STAR FACT** ★
> The 'Eternal God' redwood tree in Prairie Creek, California is 12,000 years old.

Poisonous plants

◀ *Every single part of the deadly nightshade is highly poisonous and eating a berry will kill you. But in the 1500s ladies would drop extracts in their eyes to make their eyes widen attractively, earning it the name 'belladonna'.*

- **There are thousands** of plants around the world that are poisonous at least in parts.

- **Some parts** of edible plants are poisonous, such as potato leaves and apricot and cherry stones.

- **Some plants** are toxic to eat; some toxic to touch; some create allergic reactions through the air with their pollen.

- **The rosary pea** has pretty red and black seeds often used to make bracelets. But eating one seed can kill a human.

- **Oleanders** are so poisonous that people have been killed by eating meat roasted on an oleander stick.

- **Poison ivy** inflames skin badly if touched.

- **Hemlock** belongs to the parsley family but is highly poisonous. It was said to be the plant used to kill the ancient Greek philosopher Socrates.

- **Birthwort** is a poisonous vine, but its name comes from its use in the past to help women in childbirth.

- **Crowfoots** such as aconite and hellebore, and spurges such as castor-oil and croton are poisonous.

- **Many useful drugs** are poisons extracted from plants and given in small doses including digitalis from foxgloves, morphine from poppies, atropine from deadly nightshade, quinine, aconite, strychnine and cocaine.

Ferns

- **Ferns** belong to a group of plants called feather plants or pteridophytes, along with club mosses and horsetails.

- **Featherplants** are among the world's most ancient plants, found as fossils in rocks 400 million years old.

- **Coal is made** largely of fossilized featherplants of the Carboniferous Period 360–286 million years ago.

- **There are now** 10,000 species of fern living in damp, shady places around the world.

- **Some ferns** are tiny, with mossy leaves just 1 cm long.

- **Rare tropical tree ferns** can grow up to 25m tall.

- **Fern leaves** are called fronds. When new they are curled up like a shepherd's crook, but they gradually uncurl.

- **Ferns** grow into new plants not from seeds but from spores in two stages.

- **First** spores are made in sacs called sporangia. These are the brown spots on the underside of the fronds. From these spores spread out. Some settle in suitable places.

▶ Most ferns grow on the ground in damp, shady places, but some grow on the leaves or stems of other plants.

- **Second** spores develop into a tiny heart-shaped plant called a prothallus that makes male and female cells. When bathed in rain, the male cells swim to the female cells, fertilizing them. A new root and stem then grow into a proper fern frond and the tiny prothallus dies.

Maize or corn

- **Maize or corn** is the USA's most important crop, and the second most important crop around the world after wheat. Rice is the third.

- **Corn**, like all cereals, is a kind of grass.

- **Corn** was first grown by the Indians of Mexico over 7000 year ago and so came to be called Indian corn by Europeans like Columbus.

- **In the USA** only varieties that give multi-coloured ears are now called Indian corn.

- **The Corn Belt** of the USA grows 40 percent of the world's corn.

- **American corn** grows up to 3 m tall.

- **The ear or head** of a corn plant is called a cob and is covered with tightly packed yellow or white kernels of seeds. The kernels are the part of the plant that is eaten.

◀ Ears of mature American corn are typically 20 cm or so long. The core or cob is covered with 18 rows of yellow or white kernels.

- **There are seven main kinds** of corn kernel: dent corn, flint corn, flour corn, sweet corn, popcorn, waxy corn and pod corn.

- **Some corn** is ground into flour; some is eaten whole as sweet corn; some is fed to livestock.

- **Popcorn** has no starch, unlike most other corn. When heated, moisture in the kernels turns to steam and expands or pops rapidly.

Cereals

▶ Harvesting wheat and using it to make flour is a complex process. The process is still done with simple tools in some parts of the world. But in the developed world, the entire process is largely mechanized.

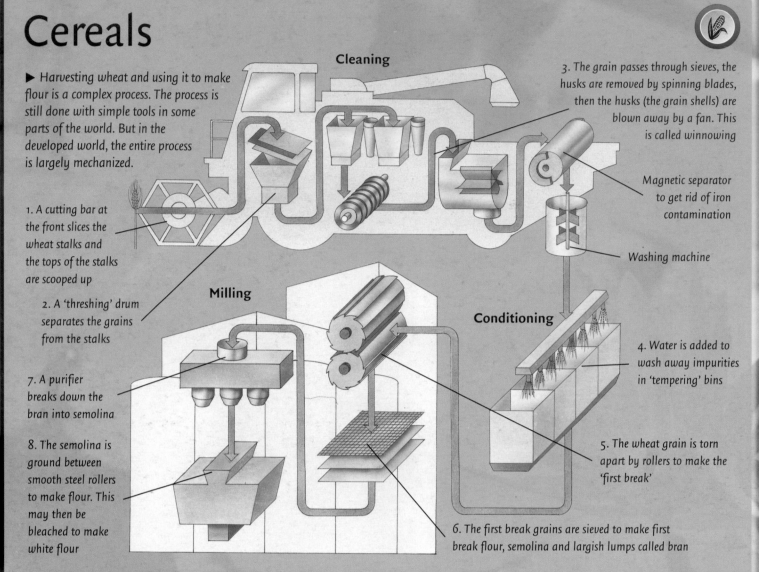

Cleaning

Milling

Conditioning

1. A cutting bar at the front slices the wheat stalks and the tops of the stalks are scooped up

2. A 'threshing' drum separates the grains from the stalks

3. The grain passes through sieves, the husks are removed by spinning blades, then the husks (the grain shells) are blown away by a fan. This is called winnowing

Magnetic separator to get rid of iron contamination

Washing machine

4. Water is added to wash away impurities in 'tempering' bins

5. The wheat grain is torn apart by rollers to make the 'first break'

6. The first break grains are sieved to make first break flour, semolina and largish lumps called bran

7. A purifier breaks down the bran into semolina

8. The semolina is ground between smooth steel rollers to make flour. This may then be bleached to make white flour

- **Cereals** such as wheat, maize, rice, barley, sorghum, oats, rye and millet are the world's major sources of food.

- **Cereals are grasses** and we eat their seeds or grain.

- **The leaves and stalks** are usually left to rot into animal feed called silage.

- **Some grains** such as rice are simply cooked and eaten. Most are milled and processed into foods such as flour, oils and syrups.

- **In the developed world** – that is, places like North America and Europe – wheat is the most important food crop. But for half the world's population, including most people in Southeast Asia and China rice is the staple food.

- **Many grains** are used to make alcoholic drinks such as whisky. A fermentation process turns the starch in the grains to alcohol. Special processing of barley creates a food called malt, which is used by brewers to make beer and lager.

- **Oats** have a higher food value than any other grain.

- **Rye** makes heavy, black bread. The bread is heavy because rye does not contain much gluten that yeast needs to make bread rise.

- **Russia** grows more oats and rye than any other country.

- **Millet** gives tiny seeds and is grown widely in dry regions of Africa and Asia. It was the main crop all over Europe, Asia and Africa in ancient and medieval times.

▶ Wheat flour is used to make everything from pasta to bread.

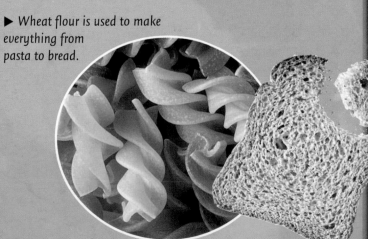

Cactus

- **Cacti** are American plants with sharp spines, thick, bulbous green stems and no leaves.

  - **Most cacti** grow in hot, dry regions but a few grow in rainforests and in cold places such as mountain tops.

  - **Cacti** in deserts have a thick, waxy skin to cut water loss to the bare minimum.

◀ The huge saguaro cactus grows only in the dry foothills and deserts of southern Arizona, southeast California and northwest Mexico.

★ STAR FACT ★
The stems of the jumping cholla fall off so easily they seem to jump on passers-by.

- **The fat stems** of cacti hold a lot of water so that they can survive in hot, dry deserts.

- **Because of their moist stems**, cacti are called succulents.

- **Cacti have spines** to protect themselves from animals which eat any moist vegetation.

- **Cacti** have to pollinate just like every flowering plant. So every few years, many produce big colourful blooms to attract insects quickly.

- **Most cacti** have very long roots to collect water from a large area. The roots grow near the surface to collect as much rainwater as possible.

- **The biggest cactus** is the saguaro, which can grow up to 20 m tall and 1 m thick.

Plankton

- **Plankton** are tiny floating organisms (living things) that are found in both the sea and ponds and lakes.

- **The word 'plankton'** comes from a Greek word meaning 'wandering'.

- **Plankton** is a general term that includes every marine organism too small and weak to swim for itself.

- **The smallest algae** are called plankton, but large floating algae (seaweeds) are not called plankton.

- **Plankton** can be divided into phytoplankton, which are tiny plants, and zooplankton, which are tiny animals, but the division is blurred.

- **Most phytoplankton** are very tiny indeed and so called nannoplankton and microplankton. Zooplankton are generally bigger and called macroplankton.

- **Green algae** that give many ponds a bright green floating carpet are plankton.

- **Phytoplankton** get their energy by photosynthesis just like other plants.

- **Countless puffs** of oxygen given out by plankton early in Earth's history gave the air its vital oxygen.

- **Plankton** is the basic food of all large ocean animals.

▼ Diatoms are at the beginning of the ocean food chain. They use the sun's energy for growth.

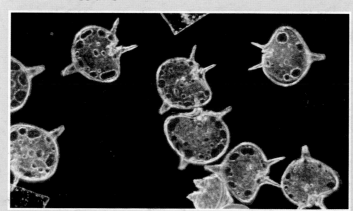

Garden flowers

▲ *Most gardens now have a mix of trees and shrubs, mixed beds of herbaceous flowers and early-flowering bulbs such as crocuses.*

- **All garden flowers** are descended from plants that were once wild, but they have been bred over the centuries to produce flowers quite unlike their wild relatives.

- **Garden flowers** such as tea roses, created by cross-breeding two different species, are called hybrids.

- **Garden flowers** tend to have much bigger blooms and last for longer than their wild cousins.

- **By hybridization** gardeners have created colours impossible naturally, such as black roses.

- **Ornamentals** are flowers cultivated just for show.

- **Gardeners** try to mix flowers that bloom at different times so that the garden is always full of colour.

- **18th century botanist** Carl Linnaeus made a clock by planting flowers that bloomed at different times of day.

- **The earliest flowerbeds** were the borders of flower tufts Ancient Persians grew along pathways.

- **A herbaceous border** is a traditional flowerbed planted with herbaceous perennial flowers like delphiniums and chrysanthemums. It flowers year after year.

> ★ STAR FACT ★
> Herbaceous borders were invented by Kew gardener George Nicolson in the 1890s.

Cocoa

- **Cocoa beans** are the fruit of the cacao tree.

- **Cocoa beans** are called cocoa beans and not cacao beans because of a spelling mistake made by English importers in the 18th century when chocolate first became popular.

- **Cocoa beans** are the seeds inside melon-shaped pods about 30 cm long.

- **Cacao trees** came originally from Central America. Now they are grown in the West Indies and West Africa too.

- **Chocolate** is made by grinding the kernels of cocoa beans to a paste called chocolate liquor. The liquor is hardened in moulds to make chocolate.

- **Cooking chocolate** is bitter. Eating chocolate has sugar and, often, milk added.

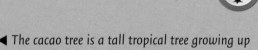

◄ *The cacao tree is a tall tropical tree growing up to about 8 m. The seeds used to make cocoa are small beans inside the melon-sized pod.*

- **Cocoa powder** is made by squeezing the cocoa butter (fat) from chocolate liquor then pulverizing it.

- **When Spanish explorer** Hernán Cortés reached the court of Moctezuma (Aztec ruler of Mexico in 1519) he was served a bitter drink called *xocoatl*. The people of Central America had regarded *xocoatl* as a sacred drink since the time of the Mayans.

- **In the 1600s** Europeans began to open fashionable chocolate houses to serve *xocoatl* as hot chocolate sweetened with sugar. In the 1700s, the English began adding milk to improve the flavour.

- **'Cacao'** is a Mayan word for 'bitter juice'; chocolate comes from the Mayan for 'sour water'.

Plants and water

- **Plants cannot survive** without water. If they are deprived of water, most plants will wilt and die very quickly – although some desert plants manage to get by on very little indeed.

- **Nearly all plants** are almost 70 percent water, and some algae are 98 percent water.

- **In plants**, water fills up the tiny cells from which they are made, and keeps them rigid in the same way as air in a balloon.

- **For a plant** water also serves the same function as blood in the human body. It carries dissolved gases, minerals and nutrients to where they are needed.

▲ Plants need regular watering to keep them fresh and healthy.

- **Some water** oozes from cell to cell through the cell walls in a process called osmosis.

- **Some water** is piped through tubes called xylem. These are the fine veins you can often see on leaves.

- **Water in xylem** is called sap and contains many dissolved substances besides water.

- **Plants lose water** by transpiration. This is evaporation through the leaf pores or stomata.

- **As water is lost** through the stomata, water is drawn up to replace it through the xylem.

- **If there is too little** water coming from the roots, the cells collapse and the plant wilts.

Algae

- **Algae** are simple organisms that live in oceans, lakes, rivers and damp mud.

- **Some algae** live inside small transparent animals.

- **Algae vary** from single-celled microscopic organisms to huge fronds of seaweed (brown algae) over 60 m long.

- **The smallest** float freely, but others, such as seaweeds, need a place to grow like a plant.

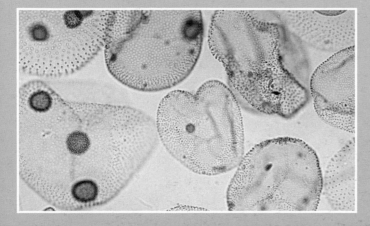

- **Algae** are so varied and often live very differently from plants, so scientists put them not in the plant kingdom but in a separate kingdom called the *Proctista*, along with slime moulds.

- **The most ancient** algae are called blue-green algae or cyanobacteria and are put in the same kingdom as bacteria. They appeared on Earth 3 billion years ago.

- **Algae** may be tiny but they are a vital food source for creatures from shrimps to whales, and they provide most of the oxygen water creatures need for life.

- **Green algae** are found mostly in freshwater. The green is the chlorophyll that enables plants to get their energy from sunlight.

- **Green algae** called *Spirogyra* form long threads.

- **Red or brown algae** are found in warm seas. Their chlorophyll is masked by other pigments.

◄ *Volvox are green algae that live in colonies about the size of a pinhead, containing up to 60,000 cells.*

Grapes

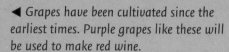

- **Grapes** are juicy, smooth-skinned berries that grow in tight clusters on woody plants called vines.

- **Grapes** can be black, blue, green, purple, golden or white, depending on the kind.

- **Some grapes** are eaten fresh and some dried as raisins, but 80 percent are crushed to make wine.

- **Grapes** are grown all round the world in places where there are warm summers and mild winters, especially in France, Italy, Spain, Australia, Chile, Romania, Georgia, South Africa and California.

- **Among the best wine grapes** are the Cabernet Sauvignon and Chardonnay for white wine and the Pinot Noir for red wine.

◄ Grapes have been cultivated since the earliest times. Purple grapes like these will be used to make red wine.

- **The ancient Egyptians** made wine from grapes 5000 years ago.

- **Grapes are made** into wine by a process called fermentation.

- **Grapes** for eating fresh are called table grapes and are bigger and sweeter than wine grapes. Varieties include Emperor, red Tokay, green Perlette and black Ribier.

- **Grapes grown** for raisins are seedless. The best known is Thompson's seedless, sometimes called the sultana.

- **Grapevines** are grown from cuttings. They start to give fruit after three or four years and may bear fruit for a century. Each vine usually gives 10–35 kg of grapes.

Growing from seed

▶ This illustration shows some of the stages of germination, as a plant grows from a seed – here a bean seed.

- **When seeds mature,** they contain the germ (embryo) of a new plant and the food needed to grow it.

- **The seed lies dormant** (inactive) until conditions are right for it to germinate (grow into a plant) – perhaps when it begins to warm up in spring.

- **Poppy seeds** can lie buried in soil for years until brought to the surface by ploughing, allowing them to grow.

- **Scientists once grew** plants from lotus seeds that were 10,000 years old.

- **A seed needs** water and warmth to germinate.

- **When a seed germinates** a root (or radicle) grows down from it and a green shoot (or plumule) grows up.

1. The seed lies dormant until conditions are right

2. The seed sends a root down and a shoot up

- **The first leaves** in the sunflower to come up are the seed-leaves or cotyledons, of which there are two.

- **Only certain parts** of a plant, called meristems, can grow. These are usually the tips of shoots and roots.

- **Because** a plant grows at the tips, shoots and roots mainly get longer rather than fatter. This is called primary growth.

- **Later in life** a plant may grow thicker or branch out.

3. The shoot bursts into the air and grows cotyledons (seed leaves)

4. The stem and roots grow longer, and the plant soon begins to grow new leaves

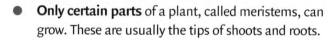
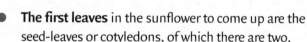

Prairie and steppe

- **Grasslands in cool parts** of the world are called prairies or steppes. There is not enough rain all year round for trees to grow.

- **Prairies** are the grasslands of North America. Steppes are the grasslands of Russia. Every region has its own name for grasslands, such as the veld in South Africa and pampas in South America. But now grasslands anywhere with tall grass are usually called prairies and grasslands with shorter grass are usually called steppes.

- **Hundreds of kinds** of grass grow in prairies. In moist areas in North America, there are grasses such as switch grass, wild rye, Indian grass and big bluestem. In drier areas, the main grasses are dropseeds, little bluestem, June grass, needlegrass and blue grama. Slough grass grows in marshland. The state of Kentucky is famous for its bluegrass.

▼ When European pioneers first saw the American prairies in the 19th century, they described them as 'a sea of grass, stretching to the horizon'. Now, corn and wheat fields and cattle ranches cover most of them. Wild prairies like this are now very rare.

- **Meadow grass** is the most common of all grasses, found on grasslands all over the world – and in garden lawns.

- **Shrubs** such as prairie roses often grow amid the grass, while oaks, cottonwoods and willows grow near rivers.

- **The many prairie flowers** include blazing stars, coneflowers, sunflowers, asters and goldenrods.

- **Eurasian grasslands** bloom with vetches, trefoils, worts, orchids and many herbs.

- **Grasslands cover** nearly a quarter of the Earth's land surface.

- **When grasslands** are destroyed by farming, the soil can be blown away by the wind as in the dust bowl of North America in the 1900s.

> ★ STAR FACT ★
> Prairies and steppes typically have very dark soils such as chernozems. The word *chernozem* is Russian for 'black earth'.

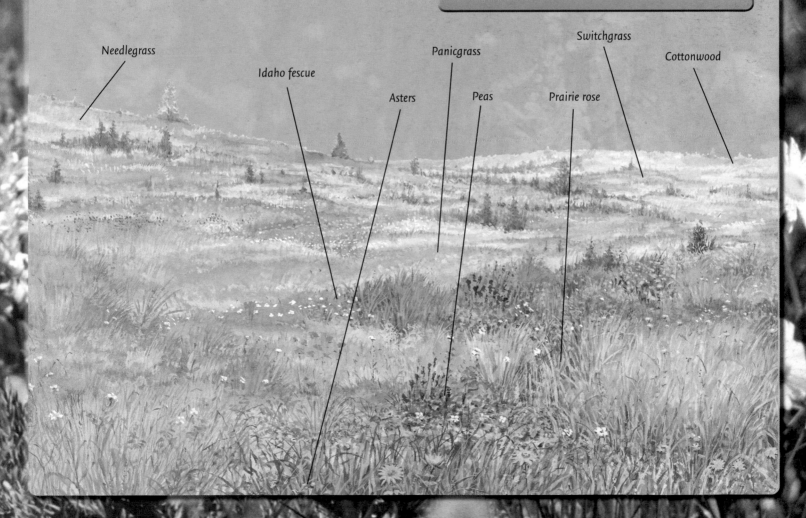

Needlegrass · Idaho fescue · Asters · Panicgrass · Peas · Prairie rose · Switchgrass · Cottonwood

Palm trees

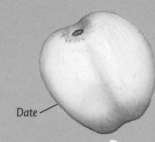

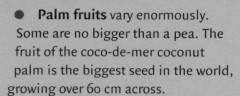

Date —

Raffia Palm

▶ Date palms produce several clusters of 600–1700 dates towards the end of the year, each year, for about 60 years.

- **Palms** are a group of 2780 species of tropical trees and shrubs.

- **Palms** have a few very large leaves called fronds.

- **The fronds** grow from the main bud at the top of a tall thin trunk.

- **If the main bud** at the top of the trunk is damaged, the tree will stop growing and die.

- **Palm trunks** do not get thicker like other trees; they simply grow taller.

- **Some palms** have trunks no bigger than a pencil; others are 60 m high and 1 m across.

- **Palm fruits** vary enormously. Some are no bigger than a pea. The fruit of the coco-de-mer coconut palm is the biggest seed in the world, growing over 60 cm across.

- **Palm trees** are a very ancient group of plants, and fossil palms have been found dating back 100 million years to the time of the dinosaurs.

- **Date palms** have been cultivated in the hottest parts of North Africa and the Middle East for at least 5000 years. Muslims regard it as the tree of life.

> ★ STAR FACT ★
> The world's largest leaves are those of the Raffia palm, which grow up to 20 m long.

Coastal plants

- **Plants** that grow on coasts must be able to cope with exposure to wind and salt spray, and thin, salty soils.

- **Plants** that can tolerate salt are called halophytes.

- **Spray halophytes** can tolerate occasional splashing.

- **True halophytes** can tolerate regular immersion when the tide comes in.

◀ Sea pinks are also known as thrift because they 'thrive' all the year round on the most exposed cliffs.

- **The annual seablite** is a true halophyte that lives in between the tides. The word 'blite' comes from an old English word for spinach.

- **The rock samphire's** name comes from St Pierre (St Peter) who was known as the rock. The plant clings to bare rock faces. Samphire was once a popular vegetable and poor people risked their lives to collect it from cliffs.

- **The droppings** of sea birds can fertilize the soil and produce dense growths of algae and weeds such as dock.

- **Lichens** on rock coasts grow in three colour bands in each tidal zone, depending on their exposure to salt.

- **Grey 'sea ivory' lichen** grows above the tide; orange lichens survive constantly being splashed by waves; black lichens grow down to the low water mark.

- **On pebble and shingle beaches** salt-tolerant plants like sea holly, sea kale and sea campion grow.

Lilies

▲ Lilies are one of the most popular garden flowers and have been cultivated in a wide range of colours.

- **Lilies** are one of the largest and most important flower families, containing about 4000 species.
- **Lilies** are monocots (which means a single leaf grows from their seeds) and give their name to the entire group of monocots – liliopsidae.

- **The lily family** includes many flowers called lilies but also asparagus and aloes.
- **Hyacinths** belong to the lily family.
- **Lilies** grow from bulbs to produce clusters of bright trumpet-shaped flowers on tall stems. Each flower has six petals.
- **Lily-of-the-valley** has tiny white bell-shaped blooms. According to superstition, anyone who plants it will die within a year.
- **Lilies-of-the-valley** are famous for their fragrance. They are used to scent soaps and perfumes.
- **Easter lilies** are large trumpet-shaped white lilies that have come to symbolize Easter.
- **Leopard lilies** grow in the western coastal states of the United States. They have red-orange flowers spotted with purple.
- **The Madonna lily** is a lily planted in August that lives throughout the winter.

Cotton

- **Cotton** is a fibre that comes from the cotton plant.
- **The cotton plant** is a small shrub that grows in tropical and subtropical climates.
- **Cotton plants** are annuals and are planted fresh each spring.
- **Cotton plants** grow seed pods called bolls, containing 20–40 seeds – each covered with soft, downy hairs or fibres.
- **As bolls ripen** they burst open to reveal the mass of fluffy fibres inside.
- **When separated** from the seeds, the fluff is known as cotton lint.
- **Cotton seeds** are processed to make oil, cattle cake and fertilizer.
- **There are 39 species** of cotton plant, but only four are cultivated: the upland, Pima, tree and Levant.
- **Upland plants** give 90 percent of the world's cotton.

▲▶ The bolls picked for cotton develop from the seed pod left when the petals of the cotton flower drop off in summer.

- **Upland** and Pima both came from the Americas, unlike tree and Levant, which are from the Middle East and Africa.

Eucalyptus trees

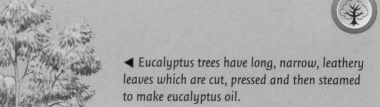

- **Eucalyptus trees** make up a group of over 400 species of Australian trees. They grow fast and straight, and often reach tremendous heights.

- **Eucalyptus trees** grow best in warm places with marked wet and dry seasons.

- **In winter** eucalyptus trees simply stop growing and produce no new buds.

- **Eucalyptus trees** in California were grown originally from seeds that came from Tasmania.

- **Australians** often call eucalyptus trees gum trees or just gums.

- **Eucalyptus leaves** give eucalyptus oil, used as vapour rubs for people with colds.

> ★ STAR FACT ★
> Eucalyptus trees can grow to over 90 m tall –
> taller than any trees but Californian redwoods.

◀ *Eucalyptus trees have long, narrow, leathery leaves which are cut, pressed and then steamed to make eucalyptus oil.*

- **The most important** tree grown for oil is the Blue mallee or blue gum. Blue gum trees are the most widespread in North America.

- **Some eucalyptus trees** give Botany Bay kino, a resin used to protect ships against worms and other animals that make holes in their hulls.

- **The jarrah** is an Australian eucalyptus that gives a red wood rather like mahogany. Other eucalyptus woods are used to make everything from boats to telegraph poles.

Green vegetables

- **Green vegetables** are the edible green parts of plants, including the leaves of plants such as cabbages and the soft stems of plants like asparagus.

- **Cabbages** are a large group of green vegetables called the brassicas.

- **Cabbages were** originally developed from the sea cabbage (*Brassica oleracea*) which grew wild near sea coasts around Europe.

- **Kale and collard** are types of cabbage with loose, open leaves.

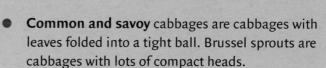

◀ *Lettuces are among the most popular green salad vegetables, used in everything from the famous 'Caesar salads' to garnishes with fast food.*

- **Common and savoy** cabbages are cabbages with leaves folded into a tight ball. Brussel sprouts are cabbages with lots of compact heads.

- **Cauliflower and broccoli** are cabbages with thick flowers. Kohlrabi is a cabbage with a bulbous stem.

- **The leaves of green vegetables** are rich in many essential vitamins including vitamin A, vitamin E and folic acid (one of the B vitamins).

- **Spinach** looks a little like kale, but it is actually a member of the goosefoot family, rich in vitamins A and C, and also in iron. The discovery of the iron content made spinach into the superfood of the cartoon hero Popeye in the mid 20th century.

- **Asparagus** belongs to the lily family. Garden asparagus has been prized since Roman times.

- **In Argenteuil** in France, asparagus is grown underground to keep it white. White asparagus is especially tender and has the best flavour.

Marshes and wetlands

- **There are two kinds of marsh:** freshwater and saltwater.
- **Freshwater marshes** occur in low-lying ground alongside rivers and lakes where the water level is always near the soil surface.
- **Freshwater marshes** are dominated by rushes, reeds and sedges.
- **Sedges** are like grass but have solid triangular stems. They grow in damp places near the water's edge.
- **Rushes** have long cylindrical leaves and grow in tussocks in damp places along the bank.
- **Reeds** are tall grasses with round stems, flat leaves and purplish flowers. They grow in dense beds in open water.
- **Free-floating** plants like duckweed and frogbit are common in marshes. In rivers they'd be washed away.
- **Water horsetails** are relics of plants that dominated the vast swamps of the Carboniferous Period some 300 million years ago.

▲ *Reeds and floating duckweed thrive in open water in marshes.*

- **Saltwater marshes** are flooded twice daily by salty seawater. Cordgrasses and salt-meadow grass are common. Reeds and rushes grow where it is least salty.
- **Where mud is firm**, glasswort and seablite take root. Further from the water sea aster and purslane grow. On high banks, sea lavender, sea plantain and thrift bloom.

Bulbs and suckers

- **Annuals and biennials** only grow once, from a seed. Many perennials die back and grow again and again from parts of the root or stem. This is called vegetative propagation.
- **Plants such as lupins** grow on the base of an old stem. As the plant ages, the stem widens and the centre dies, leaving a ring of separate plants around the outside.
  - **Plants such as irises** sprout from thick stems called rhizomes. These grow sideways beneath the ground.
    - **If the end** of a rhizome swells up it forms a lump called a tuber.
      - **Potatoes** are the tubers of the potato plant.

- **Flowers like crocuses** and gladioli have a bulbous base to their stem. This is called a corm.
- **Bulbs like those** of tulips, daffodils and onions look like corms, but they are actually made of leaf parts rather than the stem. This is why they have layers.
- **Garlic bulbs** are separated into four or five segments called cloves.
- **In winter**, rhizomes, tubers, corms and bulbs act as food stores. In spring they provide the energy to grow new leaves.
- **Plants can also** propagate (grow new plants) by sending out long stems that creep over the ground called runners or under the ground (suckers).

Bulb

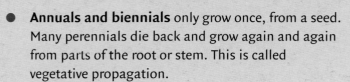

Corm

Tuber

Rhizome

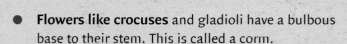

Seed dispersal

◄ *Dandelion seeds have feathery tufts that act like parachutes, whirling them away through the air as they drop to the ground.*

- **After maturing** seeds go into a period called dormancy. While they are in this state they are scattered and dispersed.

- **Some scattered seeds** fall on barren ground and never grow into plants. Only those that fall in suitable places will begin to grow.

- **Some seeds** are light enough to be blown by the wind. The feathery seed cases of some grasses are so light they can be blown several kilometres.

- **Many seeds and fruits** have wings to help them whirl through the air. Maple fruits have wings. So too do the seeds of ashes, elms and sycamores.

- **Seeds** like dandelions, cottonwoods and willows have fluffy coverings, so they drift easily on the wind.

- **Some seeds** are carried by water. Coconut seeds can float on the sea for thousands of kilometres.

- **Many fruits and seeds** are dispersed by animals.

- **Some fruits** are eaten by birds and other animals. The seeds are not digested but passed out in the animal's body waste.

- **Some seeds** stick to animal fur. They have burrs or tiny barbs that hook on to the fur, or even a sticky coating.

- **Some fruits,** like geraniums and lupins, simply explode, showering seeds in all directions.

► *Sycamore seeds have wings to help them spin away on the wind.*

Mountain plants

- **Conditions get colder,** windier and wetter higher up mountains, so plants get smaller and hardier.

- **On lower slopes** conifers such as pines, firs, spruces and larches often grow.

- **Above a certain height,** called the tree-line, it gets too cold for trees to grow.

- **In Australia,** eucalyptus trees grow near the tree-line. In New Zealand, Chile and Argentina southern beeches grow.

★ **STAR FACT** ★
On Mt Kenya in Africa, huge dandelion-like plants called giant groundsels grow as big as trees.

- **Above the tree-line** stunted shrubs, grasses and tiny flowers grow. This is called alpine vegetation.

- **Alpine flowers** like purple and starry saxifrage have tough roots that grow into crevices and split the rocks.

- **There are few insects** high up, so flowers like saxifrage and snow gentian have big blooms to attract them.

- **To make the most** of the short summers, the alpine snowbell grows its flower buds the previous summer, then lets the bud lie dormant through winter under snow.

- **Alpine flowers** such as edelweiss have woolly hairs to keep out the cold. Tasmanian daisies grow in dense cushion-shapes to keep warm.

◄ *As you go higher up a mountain, the trees of the lower slopes thin out. At the top, only mosses and lichens grow.*

Tropical grassland

- **Tropical grasslands** are regions in the tropics where there is not enough rain half the year for trees to grow.

- **Grasses** in tropical grasslands tend to grow taller and faster than grasses in cooler regions.

- **Grass stalks** may be eaten by grazing animals, burned by bush fires or dry out, but roots survive underground.

- **In Africa** grasses include 3 m-tall elephant grasses. In Australia, they include tall spear grass and shorter kangaroo grass. In South America, there are plants called bunch grasses and species such as Briza.

- **Most tropical grasslands** are scattered with bushes, shrubs and trees. In Africa, typical trees include hardy broad-leaved trees such as curatella and byrsonima.

- **Many grassland trees** are said to be sclerophyllous. This means they have tough leaves and stems to save water.

- **In drier regions** acacias and other thorn trees are armed with spines to protect them against plant-eating animals. The thorns can be up to 50 cm long.

▲ *Baobabs are East African trees with massive trunks up to 9 m across which act as water stores.*

- **In damper places** palm trees often take the place of the thorn trees.

- **In East Africa**, the grassland is called savanna, and this name is often used for tropical grassland everywhere.

- **Baobab trees** look so odd that Arab legend says the devil turned them upside down so their roots stuck up in the air.

Conifers

- **Conifers** are trees with needle-like, typically evergreen leaves that make their seeds not in flowers but in cones.

- **With gingkos and cycads** they make up the group of plants called gymnosperms, all of which make their seeds in cones.

- **The world's tallest tree**, the redwood, is a conifer.

- **The world's most massive tree**, the giant sequoia, is a conifer.

- **One of the world's oldest trees** is the bristlecone pine of California and Nevada, almost 5000 years old.

- **The world's smallest trees** are probably conifers including natural bonsai cypresses and shore pines which reach barely 20 cm when fully grown.

- **Many conifers** are cone-shaped, which helps them shed snow in winter.

- **The needle-like shape** and waxy coating of the leaves helps to save water.

- **The needles of some pines** can grow up to 30 cm long. But the biggest needles ever were those of the extinct *Cordaites*, over 1 m long and 15 cm wide.

- **Conifers** grow over most of the world, but the biggest conifer forests are in places with cold winters, such as north Siberia, northern North America and on mountain slopes almost everywhere.

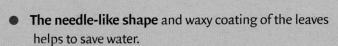

◄ *Most conifers are instantly recognizable from their conical shapes, their evergreen, needle-like leaves and their dark brown cones.*

INDEX

Entries in **bold** refer to main subject entries. Entries in *italics* refer to illustrations.